For my grandbabies: Raphael, Theodore, Otto and Leni. When I'm cooking it's like catching your hand and pressing it to my heart; taking your other hand and pressing it to your heart. It's the heat, the slightest touch, the merest tickle of skin. Four beautiful angels at my table.

PRANZO

sicilian(ish) recipes & stories guy mirabella

Hardie Grant

BOOKS

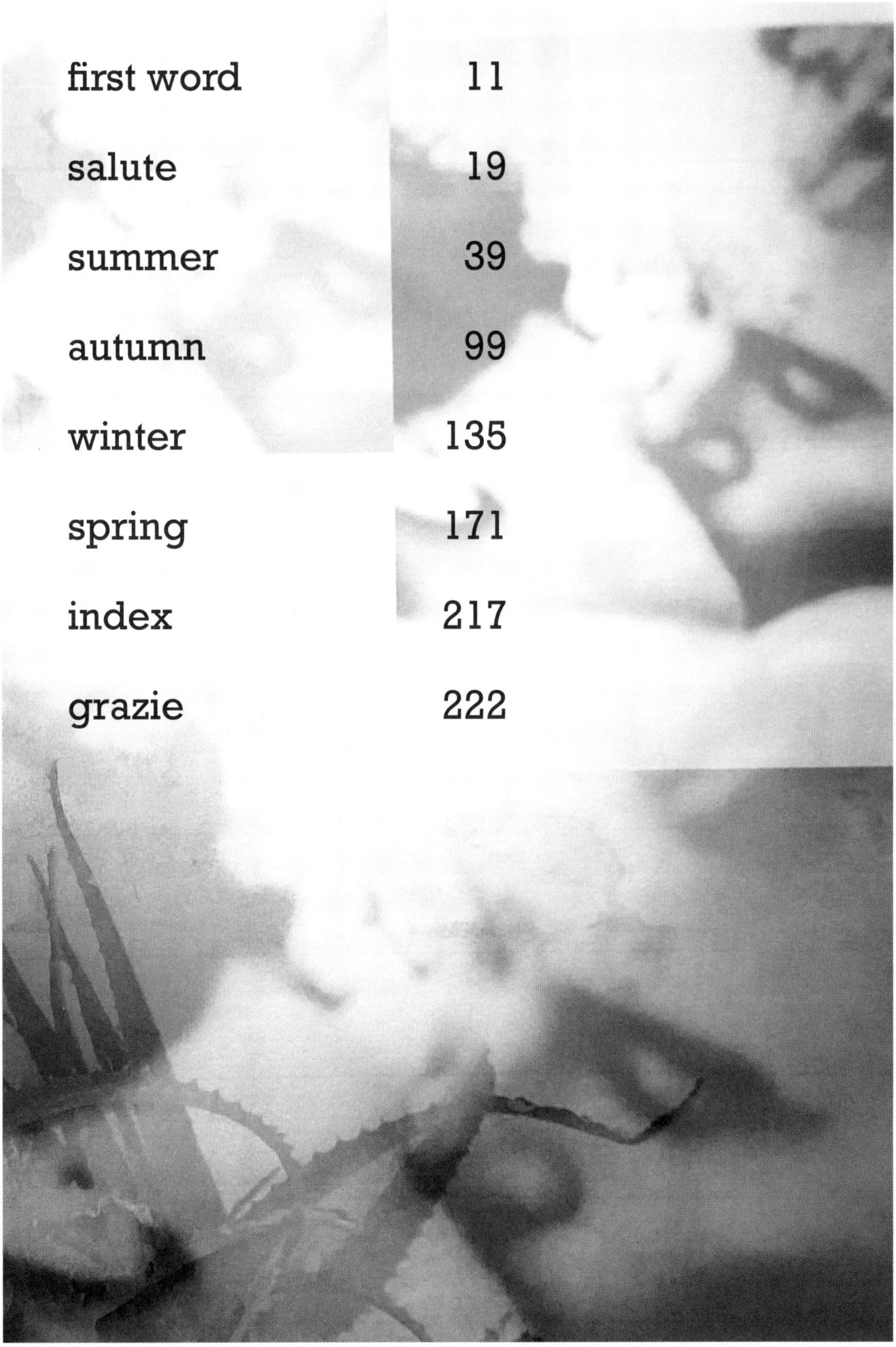

Last night I dreamt of my boyhood: Cumbrae Farm, B-52s, sea monsters, mandrills, fairground attractions, trapeze artists and silver leopards standing on brightly coloured turquoise-and-pink-striped drums. Submerged palaces of art, sleeping rooms crowded with decorative holy cards, Madonnas, Jesus and persistent kookaburras laughing in our Sicilian dialect.

My parents, Diego and Pina, were born in Calatafimi, Provincia di Trapani, Sicilia. Dad was twenty when he arrived in Australia onboard the *Ugolino Vivaldi* on 27 November 1949. Mum arrived on the 20 September 1952 on the passenger ship SS *Australia*, one of the Lloyd Triestino liners for the Australia route. Two months later, on the 22 November, they married. There was no honeymoon; they went back to the house on Barry Street, Northcote, and lived with Dad's parents – my Nonno Gaetano and Nonna Giuseppa (Giovanna) – and all of his siblings. Dad's parents had originally left Sicily in the 1880s to start a new life in New York with their families. They married there and had two children before returning to Sicily and having another six babies. After the Second World War, my grandparents moved to Australia.

From an early age, drawing and cooking have been a part of my daily routine. While my parents worked in their little fruit shop on Middleborough Road in Box Hill, I was given coloured pencils and sheets of torn butcher's paper used for wrapping fruit and vegetables to draw on, keeping me occupied and out of the way at the back of the shop. My family has always been connected to the visual; Diego and Pina made a living from having dangerously high and monumentally beautiful displays of fruit and vegetables in their shop. They spent a lot of time arranging and reimagining, gathering all kinds of ideas from found objects hanging over nearby back lanes, returning with armfuls of native flora to create works of art. These beautifully composed installations flowed like rivers between peaks – as a five-year-old they marked the beginning of my love of the visual. The magic of this little shop was heightened by its locale, nestled between two playgrounds and, crucially, opposite *il cimitero* (the cemetery). It made for a complicated mix of delight and terror. Many decades later, I now visit my Nonno and Nonna's graves across the road from our old shop.

In 1959, when I was seven years old, we moved from Box Hill to Cumbrae Farm in Tyabb, just outside Melbourne. It was an isolated place and a chance to create our own little world. Sitting at a big wooden table I would watch Mum and Nonna cook while I made pictures covered in splodges of paint, olive oil, *brodo* (broth) and red sauce.

Many of my favourite recipes come from Sunday *pranzo*; lunch at Cumbrae Farm was surrounded by Italian flavours with all roads leading to Sicily. The food I love to eat and make is layered with Sicilian heritage and history. I grew up hearing the call to lunch: *pranzo e pronto, mangia bello, mangia bella, mangia angeli alla mia tavola.*

This is not simply a book of Sicilian recipes. *Pranzo* aims to inspire your excitement about cooking, to help you feel the food at the end of your fingertips – because cooking is good for you. The easiest comparison I can make is the feeling of joy and familiarity I get from drawing, painting or designing a book. This combination of words, images and cooking have fuelled an integration of work, life, kitchen and studio – the lines of what it means to be multilingual are blurred. I've been cooking for a long time, starting at Cumbrae Farm. I was probably five when I started finger spelling in the flour at the edge of Mum's pasta-making, like plaster dust creeping its way closer to tubes of paint. Sipping coffee from gilt-edged espresso cups on the veranda with Sicilian playing cards, a kaleidoscope of colours courtesy of the kitsch Sicilian gifts from newly arrived cousins. My work is multilingual – it's the work, it's always been about the work. It's pluralistic, yet always leads back to Sicily.

I am a home cook with no chef credentials. I write recipes for the food I grew up eating and those prepared at my cafe. I studied graphic design, specialising in publication and book design, and taught for many years before pursuing a full-time career as a cafe owner, where I worked with a beautiful bunch of misfits, mainly creative types, bundled together with all sorts of coloured ribbons.

Pranzo had its origin in my home kitchen during the first Melbourne lockdown. In hospitality, you work on the premise: build it and they will come. While contemplating how to move forward with my cafe business amid the pandemic, I began to cook simple, quick recipes and post them on Instagram accompanied with little stories from my childhood. After the first month, I had so many comments suggesting I turn the recipes into a book that I began to collate them.

This book is written for my grandbabies who are always hungry and wanting more of their grandmother Jojo's *brodo* (broth), my *sfinci* (Sicilian donuts), or roasted cauliflower and pea pesto with pasta – as long as Jojo makes it.

Cooking notes | I use Australian measurements in this book.
A standard cup is 250 ml (8½ fl oz), a tablespoon is 20 ml (¾ fl oz)
and teaspoon is 5 ml (⅛ fl oz). The recipes were tested using
a fan-forced oven. If using a conventional oven, increase the
temperature by 20°C (35°F).

Flour, or its alternative, is the heartbeat of a dish.
Self-raising flour can be made by sifting together 150 g (5½ oz/1 cup)
of plain (all-purpose) flour with 1½ teaspoons of baking powder.

As a rule, I use a mild olive oil for cooking and extra-
virgin olive oil – with its distinctive rich colour and peppery
taste – for dressings or as a last-minute drizzle just before
serving. My father, Diego, always made a very simple, quick
meal to whet the appetite while the pasta was cooking. He poured
extra-virgin olive oil into a pasta bowl, then added a few drops
of his homemade vinegar – usually the last season's homemade
wine, then seasoned with salt and freshly ground black pepper.
Beside it was a bowl of cos (romaine) lettuce from the garden,
rinsed and separated so that each crisp leaf starting from the
stem end was then dipped into the dressing.

For seasoning, I use cooking salt and freshly ground
black pepper unless otherwise mentioned. I love really flaky
salt sprinkled over the top of dishes just as I'm about to serve
bruschetta and toasties. Sometimes over the top of sweets.

Finally, I have used large (60 g/2 oz) free-range eggs
for the recipes in *Pranzo*.

THIS IS THE USUAL SHIT

Brodo is the best place to start. For me, it is a word soaked in the light of our sun-drenched kitchen at Cumbrae Farm.

Taking care of the chooks and making *brodo* (broth) were my Nonna Giuseppa's passions. Displayed hanging above the stovetop were her large pots. Over the years Nonna Giuseppa lived with us, she became more hen-like – resembling the round, velvety black chooks that scratched under the fruit trees. Her wobbly hugs entwined us with the smell of *brodo* deep in her thick cooking smock.

Nothing gives my wife Jojo more joy than to make this dish for our grandbabies Raphael, Theodore, Otto and Leni. *Brodo* brings them racing to the table. *Brodo* is love in a bowl, especially when tiny star-shaped pasta is cooked in it. Whenever anyone mentions leftover *brodo* chicken, bow your head and make the sign of the cross.

Cook a handful of tortellini for each person in enough *brodo* to cover them. Take off the heat, divide between plates, add warm shredded *brodo* chicken, slow down and restore the richness of the simple things we do every day.

jojo's brodo

1 × 1.5 kg (3 lb 5 oz) organic chicken, rinsed

2 large brown onions, chopped into chunks

4 carrots, skins on, chopped into large chunks

½ bunch celery, including leafy tops

½ bunch flat-leaf (Italian) parsley

140 g (5 oz/⅔ cup) tomato paste
  (concentrated puree)

1 kg (2 lb 3 oz) small potatoes, halved

80 ml (2½ fl oz/⅓ cup) mild olive oil

grated zest of 1 lemon

1 long red chilli, finely chopped

200 g (7 oz) pastina or orzo

salt and white pepper

enough for 4–6

Put the chicken in a large heavy-based saucepan with 7 litres (236 fl oz) of water and bring to the boil, skimming off the scum that floats to the surface. Reduce the heat slightly, but maintain a gentle bubbling. Add the onions, carrots, celery, parsley, tomato paste, salt and pepper and cook for 1 hour. Check the seasoning.

Add the potatoes and cook for 20 minutes more, or until tender. Remove the potatoes with a slotted spoon and put them into a serving bowl. While still hot, add the olive oil to the potatoes and season with salt and lots of white pepper. Add the lemon zest and chilli and toss. Cover loosely with aluminium foil and keep warm, ready to serve with the chicken.

Remove the chicken from the *brodo* and strain the liquid through a colander into another large saucepan. You should have about 3 litres (101 fl oz) of *brodo*. The chicken can be left on the bone and broken into portions or shredded off the bone and placed into a serving dish with the carrots. Cover loosely with aluminium foil and keep warm.

Meanwhile, reheat half the *brodo* in a smaller saucepan, add the pastina and cook until it is al dente. If you like it more soupy, add extra *brodo* at the beginning.

The *brodo* with pastina is always served as a first course, followed by the chicken with carrots alongside the bowl of warm potato salad.

—

This recipe was passed down to Jojo from her mother, who always used white pepper in her cooking. My mother-in-law's kitchen smelt of white pepper – that's how I remember it. I seldom use white pepper, but when I do, the scent always reminds me of her.

Diego and Pina were in their late twenties with three children when they arrived at Cumbrae Farm in the spring of 1959. Josie, the youngest of the three, was just six weeks old when they made the move, while my younger brother, Frank, was six. My father's parents, my Nonno Gaetano and Nonna Giuseppa, came for a short time while we settled in. This was the year I learnt how to ride a bike, tie my shoelaces, saw chooks and other farm animals being killed, shot my first and only rabbit and drew the first sketches and paintings of Segesta, a doric temple just 6.3 km from our village of Calatafimi in Sicily.

Segesta dates back to the middle of the 5th century BC and was featured among our collection of Sicilian kitsch, which included religious posters, holy cards, travel postcards, teaspoons, tea towels, souvenir ashtrays, ceramic dishes and candle holders, egg and coffee cups painted with prickly pears and *carretto siciliano* (miniature colourful donkey-drawn carts). The colourful scenes painted on the side of these carts portrayed historical events and portraits of kings and queens. Even today a mule- or donkey-drawn *carretto* is the preferred choice of transport for carting goods. The curious, disparate mix of adornments inside the house at Cumbrae Farm was a delicious, over-the-top, palazzo-style of decoration.

On 21 June 1962, Bert Stern took the last studio portraits of Marilyn Monroe, six weeks before her tragic death. I shot this image in June 2013 at Calatafimi. Marilyn is taped to the front door of an abandoned house. I could never have anticipated a configuration of two bold and very different graphic images revamped and united in such a brilliant way. It encapsulates the best kind of Sicilian discovery – drifting down a quiet village street at midday, during *pranzo*, surrounded by ancient gardens, hearing whispers through rose-printed lace curtains, the smell of freshly cooked tomato sauce and basil everywhere.

In June 1967, I heard the American pop song 'San Francisco – Be sure to wear flowers in your hair' for the first time. In the Sicilian autumn of that year my family arrived by Lloyd Triestino SS *Guglielmo Marconi* to visit relatives, and the sound of that song was stuck in my head. Charles Dickens described Victorian London as a magic lantern with inspirational powers. Likewise, this visit to Sicily lit a fire in me: mine became a life seen in visuals. The people, the architecture, the history of the Trinacria. It was a paradise of romantic images coming together in one coalescent moment where I experienced the exasperatingly ugly at the same time as the completely engrossing and beautiful.

Mum trained in Calatafimi under the mentorship of
Signor Marchese, the village tailor, and her first job in Australia
was as a seamstress at the Holeproof factory in Box Hill. As
a young bride, the move to the Mornington Peninsula was an
unexpected interruption to the dreams she had leaving Sicily.

My father's mother, my Nonna Giuseppa, helped to
settle the family at Cumbrae Farm. Nonna, who had moved from
Sicily to New York with her family in the late 1800s and cooked in
Italian restaurants in the Bronx as a young woman in the 1900s,
helped Mum embrace cooking as another fulfilling creative outlet.
Mum gradually accumulated decades of cooking knowledge, and
was able to transform even the humblest ingredients: bread
rubbed with extra-virgin olive oil, roasted whole in the oven, then
pressed and pulled apart. We ate peppered broken bread with
stuffed semi-dried (sun-blushed) tomatoes, anchovies and chunks
of pecorino for supper every Monday night while watching *World
Championship Wrestling*. A triumph of *cucina povera*.

—

pangrattato | In a frying pan, heat 2 tablespoons extra-virgin olive oil over low heat, then
add 60 g (2 oz/1 cup) Japanese breadcrumbs, 2 crushed garlic cloves and 3–4 chopped stems
(no leaves) flat-leaf (Italian) parsley until the crumbs start to go golden brown. Take off the heat,
transfer to a bowl. Add the finely chopped tops from the flat-leaf parsley, 65 g (2¼ oz) freshly
grated pecorino and freshly ground black pepper and stir to combine. Makes 1 cup (80 g/2¾ oz).

stuffed semi-dried tomatoes with broken bread | Preheat the oven to 180°C (360°F). Place
12 Semi-dried (sun-blushed) tomatoes (page 80) on a baking tray. Top each tomato with a heaped
tablespoon of *Pangrattato* (above). Roast the stuffed tomatoes and a whole loaf of sourdough
bread in the oven for 20–30 minutes, until golden. Break the bread apart and drizzle it with
extra-virgin olive oil and season with freshly ground black pepper. Serve with salty anchovies
from a can. Enough for 4–6 people.

tomatoes

I come from a family that makes sauce with tomatoes from the garden as soon as they are ripe. The freshness holds the scent of summer.

Not that long ago, the tomato was a hardy weed on a South American mountainside. When it made its way to Europe it scandalised polite society – of course, polite society is always pretty easy to scandalise. They called the mystery *pomodoro* the 'devil's fruit', thinking it was poisonous because of its association with a group of nightshade plants. The tomato was loathed by the French aristocracy, in particular, who held that the colour red was deemed the most unflattering thing a *société polie* could wear. However, this didn't stop *Solanum lycopersicum* from becoming popular and it was soon adored by the lower classes of Europe. The French revolutionaries deemed it their food of choice: to demonstrate their unquestionable devotion to the rebellion, they chose to wear red and redefine the nature of political power.

One day I want to stand in front of Titian's *Venus and Cupid with a Partridge*, c. 1550, in the Uffizi Gallery in Florence, with its bold vermillion drapery signifying happiness, fertility and love, while I gently nudge away a tourist with my walking stick.

fresh tomato sauce 1 | Heat 80 ml (2½ fl oz/⅓ cup) extra-virgin olive oil in a large saucepan over low heat, add 1 large finely chopped brown onion and gently fry until soft, about 4 minutes. Add 2 sliced garlic cloves and fry for 1 extra minute. Season with salt, then add 1.5 kg (2 lb 5 oz) roughly chopped tomatoes, 4 teaspoons white (granulated) sugar and 250 ml (8½ fl oz/1 cup) of water. Slowly bring to the boil, then cook on a low–medium heat for 35–45 minutes, stirring occasionally to stop the sauce sticking to the bottom of the pan. Leave as is for that lovely rustic texture, pass through a mouli, or blend with a hand-held blender, resulting in a smooth sauce. Add a handful of fresh basil leaves to serve. Makes 800 ml (27 fl oz/3¼ cups).

fresh tomato sauce 2 | Wash 3 kg (6 lb 10 oz) ripe tomatoes. Cut a cross on the bottom of each tomato. Blanch the tomatoes in boiling water for 1 minute, then plunge them into cold water. With a sharp knife, remove the stems, then peel the skin. Scoop out the seeds with a knife or teaspoon. Roughly chop the tomatoes. Heat 80 ml (2½ fl oz/⅓ cup) extra-virgin olive oil in a large saucepan over low heat, add 1 large finely chopped brown onion and gently fry until soft, about 4 minutes. Add 3 sliced garlic cloves and cook for 1 minute. Season with salt, then add the chopped tomatoes, 2 teaspoons white (granulated) sugar and 250 ml (8½ fl oz/1 cup) of water. Slowly bring to the boil, then cook on a low–medium heat for 45–60 minutes, stirring occasionally to stop the sauce sticking to the bottom of the pan. Leave as is for that lovely rustic texture, pass through a mouli, or blend with a hand-held blender, resulting in a smooth sauce. Add a handful of fresh basil leaves to serve. Makes 1.2 litres (41 fl oz/5 cups).

passata sauce | Heat 80 ml (2½ fl oz/⅓ cup) extra-virgin olive oil in a large saucepan over low heat, add 1 large finely chopped brown onion and gently fry until soft, about 4 minutes. Add 2 sliced garlic cloves and fry for 1 minute. Season with salt, then add 2 × 700 g (1 lb 9 oz) jars of tomato passata (pureed tomatoes), plus 500 ml (17 fl oz/2 cups) of water, 2 tablespoons white (granulated) sugar and 30 g (1 oz/1 cup) basil leaves. Slowly bring to the boil, then cook on a low–medium heat for 45–60 minutes, stirring occasionally to stop the sauce sticking to the bottom of the pan. Leave as is for that lovely rustic texture, pass through a mouli, or blend with a hand-held blender, resulting in a smooth sauce. Add a handful of basil leaves and leave them in the sauce. You can remove them just before serving with pasta. Makes 1.4 litres (47 fl oz/5½ cups).

tinned tomato sauce | Heat 80 ml (2½ fl oz/⅓ cup) extra-virgin oil in a large saucepan over low heat, then add 1 large finely chopped brown onion, 1 finely chopped carrot and 1 finely chopped celery stalk and gently fry until the onion is soft, around 5 minutes. Season with salt, then add 3 crushed garlic cloves and 3 tablespoons tomato paste (concentrated puree) and stir thoroughly. Add a handful of mixed herbs, such as fresh oregano, rosemary and basil, then add 4 × 400 g (14 oz) tinned finely chopped tomatoes and 2 tablespoons white (granulated) sugar. Fill two of the tins with water and add this to the saucepan. Slowly bring to the boil, then cook on a low–medium heat for 45–60 minutes, stirring occasionally to stop the sauce sticking to the bottom of the pan. Leave as is, pass through a mouli, or blend with a hand-held blender, then add 2–3 tablespoons more fresh herbs, whole or chopped. Makes 2 litres (68 fl oz/8 cups).

raw tomato sauce | This is a raw tomato sauce of chopped ripe, fleshy tomatoes or halved cherry tomatoes combined with fresh basil leaves from the garden. Wash 1 kg (2 lb 3 oz) ripe tomatoes. Cut a cross on the bottom of each tomato. Blanch the tomatoes in boiling water for 1 minute, then plunge them into cold water. With a sharp knife, remove the stems, then peel the skin. Scoop out the seeds with a teaspoon. Roughly chop the tomatoes, then set aside in a bowl. If you are using cherry tomatoes there's no need to blanch; leave them whole or halve. In a food processor, blend 4 chopped garlic cloves, 1 teaspoon salt and a good handful of basil leaves. Add 125 ml (4 fl oz/½ cup) extra-virgin olive oil, then blend again. Add more oil if you think it is too dry. Add to the tomatoes and stir. You can add this sauce to a fish or chicken tray bake, marinating it overnight in the sauce. Makes 800 ml (27 fl oz/3¼ cups).

spaccare tomato sauce | *Spaccare* means to break. Wash 700 g (1 lb 9 oz) ripe tomatoes, cut off the stems, then gently squeeze and break them in half. Put them into a serving dish with the juice and seeds. Add 2 sliced garlic cloves, season with a little salt and sprinkle 1 tablespoon of rinsed Sicilian capers over the top. Add a good handful of basil leaves, 2–3 mint leaves, and, finally, a good splash of extra-virgin olive oil – not the everyday one used for cooking, the other, more assertive, prickly and peppery one, to bring out the Sicilian in you. Use as a pasta sauce or have it with roasted or fresh, torn rustic bread and salty anchovies from a can. Alternately, add it to a fish or chicken tray bake, marinating it overnight in the sauce. Makes 800 ml (27 fl oz/ 3¼ cups).

herbs

I use an enormous number of fresh herbs in my cooking. They are a constant companion on my kitchen bench and grow everywhere in my garden. Ancient Greeks covered their tombs in vibrantly green wreaths of parsley. In the Middle Ages, parsley became popular and was grown in monasteries and royal gardens. Sprigs of dill were hung from front doors and children's cradles to prevent harm. Nonna Giuseppa always said herbs help the digestive system.

Parsley and dill have a way of sweet-talking any dish, using their magic to weave flavour. And everyone stands tall when the warm bay leaf brings its natural swagger and restoration for the soul.

Fresh basil from the garden is far from discreet; its aroma haunts every room in the house, defending its existence for days. Combined with flat-leaf (Italian) parsley and almonds in *maccarruni alla Trapanese* (Trapani tomato pesto), it brings a rush of images of all the kitchens I have ever cooked in raining over my head like aromatic drops of herby perfume. The pesto's golden brown colour and toasted nutty flavour adds another layer of unbroken promises, dipped in precious oil, transported to distant shores in an Egyptian garden several centuries earlier to cultivate a lost maze of memory.

trapanese pesto | Combine 2 sliced garlic cloves, 155 g (5½ oz/1 cup) whole lightly toasted almonds, 30 g (1 oz/1 cup) basil leaves, 10 g (¼ oz/½ cup) flat-leaf (Italian) parsley, 3 tablespoons mild olive oil and a pinch of salt in a food processor and pulse to a course texture. Transfer to a bowl and add 250 g (9 oz) of roughly chopped and whole cherry tomatoes. Serve immediately with pasta. Makes 750 ml (25½ fl oz/3 cups).

basil and spinach pesto | Combine 2 sliced garlic cloves, a pinch of salt, 155 g (5½ oz/1 cup) lightly toasted pine nuts, 90 g (3 oz) freshly grated pecorino, 120 g (4½ oz/4 cups) basil leaves, 180 g (6½ oz/4 cups) baby English spinach leaves and 185 ml (6 fl oz/¾ cup) mild olive oil in a food processor and pulse in 5 second bursts until you have a coarse to smooth texture. To store, spoon into a jar or airtight container and top with 1 tablespoon of olive oil before sealing to prevent browning. Refrigerate for up to 2 days or freeze for up to 2 months. Makes 560 ml (19 fl oz/2¼ cups).

jojo's pea pesto | Heat 2 tablespoons of mild olive oil in a large saucepan over low heat, then add 1 small finely chopped brown onion and fry until translucent, about 5 minutes. Add 500 g (1 lb 2 oz) fresh or frozen peas, 250 ml (8½ fl oz/1 cup) *Jojo's brodo* (page 21), chicken stock or water and season with salt and pepper. Bring to the boil, then remove from the heat. Add 2 chopped garlic cloves and a good handful of basil and use a hand-held blender to puree until smooth. To store, spoon into a jar or airtight container. No olive oil is required for the top. Refrigerate for up to 1 week or freeze for up to 2 months. Makes 875 ml (29½ fl oz/3½ cups).

broccoli pesto | Cut the stalks off 500 g (1 lb 2 oz) broccoli. Peel the stalks and chop them into chunks. Break the broccoli heads into florets and cook in boiling water with the stalks until tender, about 3 minutes. Plunge them into cold water to stop further cooking. Combine 2 sliced garlic cloves, a pinch of salt, 35 g (1¼ oz/¼ cup) lightly toasted pistachios and 45 g (1½ oz) freshly grated pecorino in a food processor and pulse to a rough texture. Add the cooled broccoli, 60 g (2 oz/2 cups) basil leaves, 90 g (3 oz/2 cups) baby English spinach leaves, 125 ml (4 fl oz/½ cup) mild olive oil and pulse until not quite smooth. To store, spoon into a jar or airtight container and top with 1 tablespoon of olive oil before sealing to prevent browning. Refrigerate for up to 2 days or freeze for up to 2 months. Makes 700 ml (23½ fl oz/2¾ cups).

rocket pesto | Combine 2 sliced garlic cloves, a pinch of salt, 80 g (2¾ oz/½ cup) lightly toasted pine nuts, 80 g (2¾ oz/4 cups) rocket (arugula), 30 g (1 oz/1 cup) basil leaves, 10 g (¼ oz/½ cup) flat-leaf (Italian) parsley, 45 g (1½ oz) freshly grated pecorino and 125 ml (4 fl oz/½ cup) mild olive oil in a food processor and pulse in 5 second bursts until you have a coarse to smooth texture. To store, spoon into a jar or airtight container and top with 1 tablespoon olive oil before sealing to prevent browning. Refrigerate for up to 2 days or freeze for up to 2 months. Makes 310 ml (10½ fl oz/1¼ cups).

pasta

At Cumbrae Farm, dried pasta was clearly the choice for everyday cooking, while making fresh pasta was for grand occasions. Mum's creamy translucent sheets of lasagne hung on broomsticks or the backs of chairs. Tortellini and ravioli were made for really special occasions like Easter and Christmas and ricotta cannelloni with red sauce for birthdays. Maccarruni is the main culprit of *pranzo* that I return to again and again to find my Sicilian-ness.

flour and water dough | Put 400 g (14 oz/2⅔ cups) plain (all-purpose) flour or tipo 00 flour in a large bowl and make a well in the centre. Add 250 ml (8½ fl oz/1 cup) of lukewarm water. Using a fork or the tips of your fingers, begin to stir in the flour from the inside and gradually incorporate more flour to form a rough textured ball. Place the dough onto a lightly floured surface and knead for 8 minutes, until smooth. Cover the dough with a clean tea towel and rest for 30 minutes. Serves 4–6.

semolina and water dough | Put 400 g (14 oz/3¼ cups) semolina flour in a large bowl and make a well in the centre. Add 250 ml (8½ fl oz/1 cup) of lukewarm water. Using a fork or the tips of your fingers, begin to stir in the flour from the inside and gradually incorporate more flour to form a rough textured ball. Place the dough onto a surface lightly floured with semolina flour and knead for 8 minutes, until smooth. Cover the dough with a clean tea towel and rest for 30 minutes. Serves 4–6.

tipo 00 and eggs | Put 400 g (14 oz/2⅔ cups) tipo 00 flour in a large bowl and make a well in the centre. Add 4 eggs and a pinch of salt. Using a fork or the tips of your fingers, begin to stir in the flour from the inside and gradually incorporate to form a rough textured ball. Place the dough onto a surface lightly floured with tipo 00 flour and knead for 8 minutes, until smooth. Cover the dough with a clean tea towel and rest for 30 minutes. Serves 4–6.

There's something about maccarruni or busiate
that elevates the spirit, like walking into one of those beautiful
restaurants with terrazzo floors and blonde bentwood chairs
where layers of flavour wake up the senses. If there's a dish
that's most often associated with Cumbrae and the west coast
of Sicily, it's freshly made maccarruni. Making maccarruni is
like painting using only a few, bright primary colours – yellow,
blue and green – leaving lots of white space with splodges of red
creating minimal gestures. I want to eat this twizzled handmade
pasta every Sunday for *pranzo*. It has so many things I love.
I especially love it teamed with a quick, fresh tomato sauce and
roasted chunks of eggplant (aubergine) served with freshly grated
ricotta salata. Like two like-minded friends: the sweet, salty acidic
zing from the tomatoes and the nutty, creamy texture from the
eggplant, who, as usual, gets its own way.

Corkscrew maccarruni is traditionally shaped
using *buso* – the dried stem of a local grass (*Ampelodesmos
mauritanicus*) surrounding Calatafimi. All nonnas in the province
of Trapani made maccarruni with just flour and water, sometimes
a little salt and extra-virgin olive oil. Nonna Giuseppa brought
buso to Australia hidden in the pockets of her dress. Nonna's
pockets were also handy for holding pencils and scraps of paper
for jotting ingredients, Irish Moss lollies (secretly snuck to us
children behind adult eyes), seeds of various kinds and a little
sewing kit. Sometimes I wondered if Nonna kept her beloved

chooks in her large pockets. The *buso* Nonna brought with
her have survived to this day. They mean so much more than
gathered grass.

One of the most interesting features of maccarruni
is not only its long, twisting, slippery shape, but the secrets in its
ridges. It carries a personal connection to the homeland: stories
of grand picnics and celebrations at country houses filled with the
activity of summer. This fabulous handmade, twisted pasta made
with dry grass stems is awe-inspiring. The *buso* I use have been
twirled by Nonna Giuseppa and Mum's hands. The glowing patina
has a tactility mellowed by age that makes them an essential tool
for making my maccarruni.

As well as maccarruni with a red sauce, I cut
maccarruni into short twists to make casarecce, serving it with
mushroom ragu.

Every New Year's Eve, *maccarruni cu l'agghia* is
served – a sauce made with a ton of raw garlic teamed with
basil, extra-virgin olive oil and, sometimes, roughly chopped ripe
tomatoes. It's seductive but not in a rude way. I love slurping it!
It's about the visual in a naughty way.

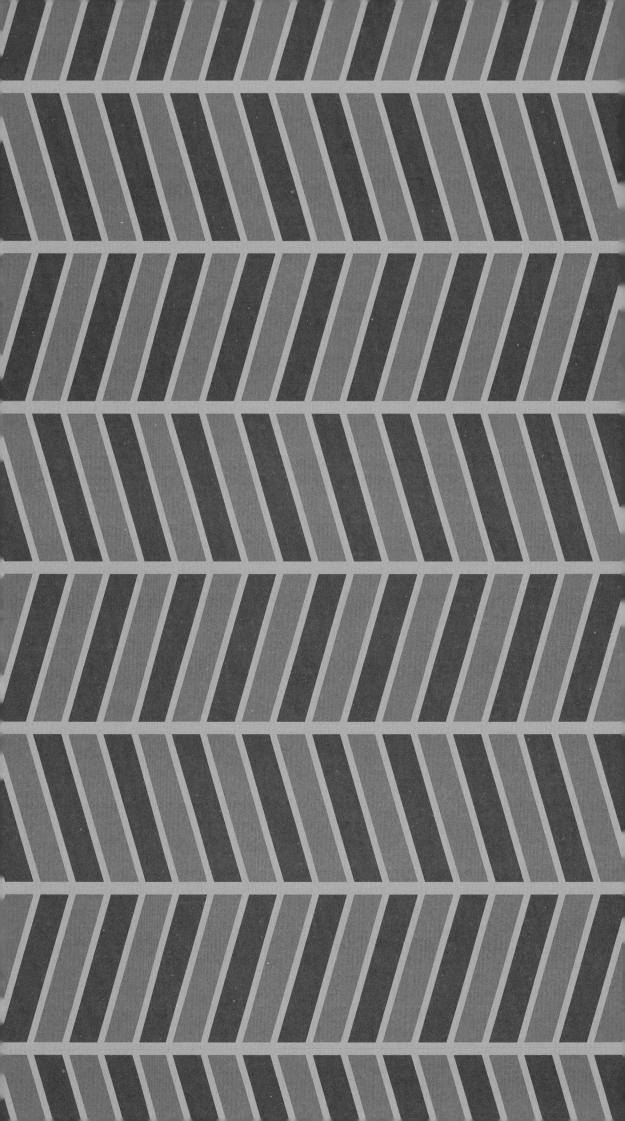

STATUS
INVITER

Carro Siciliano

Dear Raphael, Theodore, Otto and Leni, summer is my favourite season. At Cumbrae the grapevine and blood red rose cast spells over the pergola. Beetles, caterpillars and flying oysters dropped on our heads as we ran screaming underneath their shadow. Did you know there is an Australian beetle called Shiny Black Rhinoceros (*Xylotrupes ulysses*)? It is very, very big at 7 cm (2¾ in) long. The inquisitive rosellas were like rainbows in pursuit of their dreams, living on the silver tops of flowering gums, having random conversations, performing peculiar, creative acts while darting with vitality.

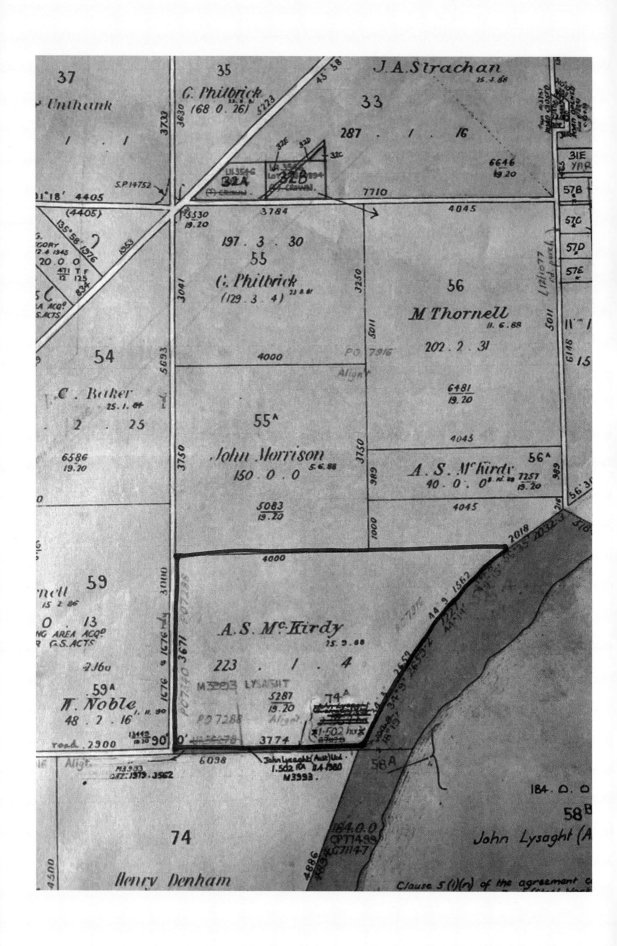

It was summer when we drove from Box Hill to our new home in McKirdys Road in Tyabb. We drove through apple orchards imagining our new home until finally we reached the narrow dirt road to the farm gate. It was framed by carpets of tall, reedy wildflowers in striped carmine pinks and pale blues. Clumps of faded lemon jonquils immune to the sagging of time added to the mood as they sank into the ground around the wooden gate. The tired, crushed-earth driveway was flanked by radiata pine trees: a contingent of infantry standing tall – on guard and serving the dual purpose of windbreak and sunless avenue. A Monterey cypress (*Cupressus macrocarpa Lambertiana*), planted in 1902 to mark the coronation of King Edward VII, stood at the end of the driveway. The gloom of an old garden formed a green cloister in front of it, framing a little wooden house built in 1930 (the original homestead was demolished in 1927).

We spent our first night sleeping in our black '48 Buick sedan under the broad arms of the enormous cypress. I fell asleep to the sound of whispering owls and my father's hushed tones, anxious to plant his tomato seedlings wrapped in the wet news of the day.

That night there was an endless line of ghosts, who with little theatricality, released a fragrant gust of mist every time they flew past – dropping big green apples on the dirt road leading up to the farm gate at the other end of the avenue. I have flashbacks of sleeping under a Mars Black night: keeping guard were the enormous cypress and Roman emperors in ecclesiastical dress with white silk zucchettos wearing bright yellow puffer jackets, accumulating knowledge of Greek origin, asking questions in search of the meaning of life.

Sometimes childhood memories are enclosed in this idyllic, protective place. I wasn't one of those kids sitting beside the radio listening to *Biggles* or the *Children's Hour*, which in its former glory was called *The Argonauts*. I was led by my eyes. The visual has always been my instrument of discovery. If I'm still making books in my nineties, it will help to lie under the branches of the cypress and visit the avenue of memories from my little boy's country life. Steeped in daydreaming and the collected impressions of a rural, natural, untamed beauty nestled at the edge of a secluded corner on Bagge Harbour – it was a good place to crash-land.

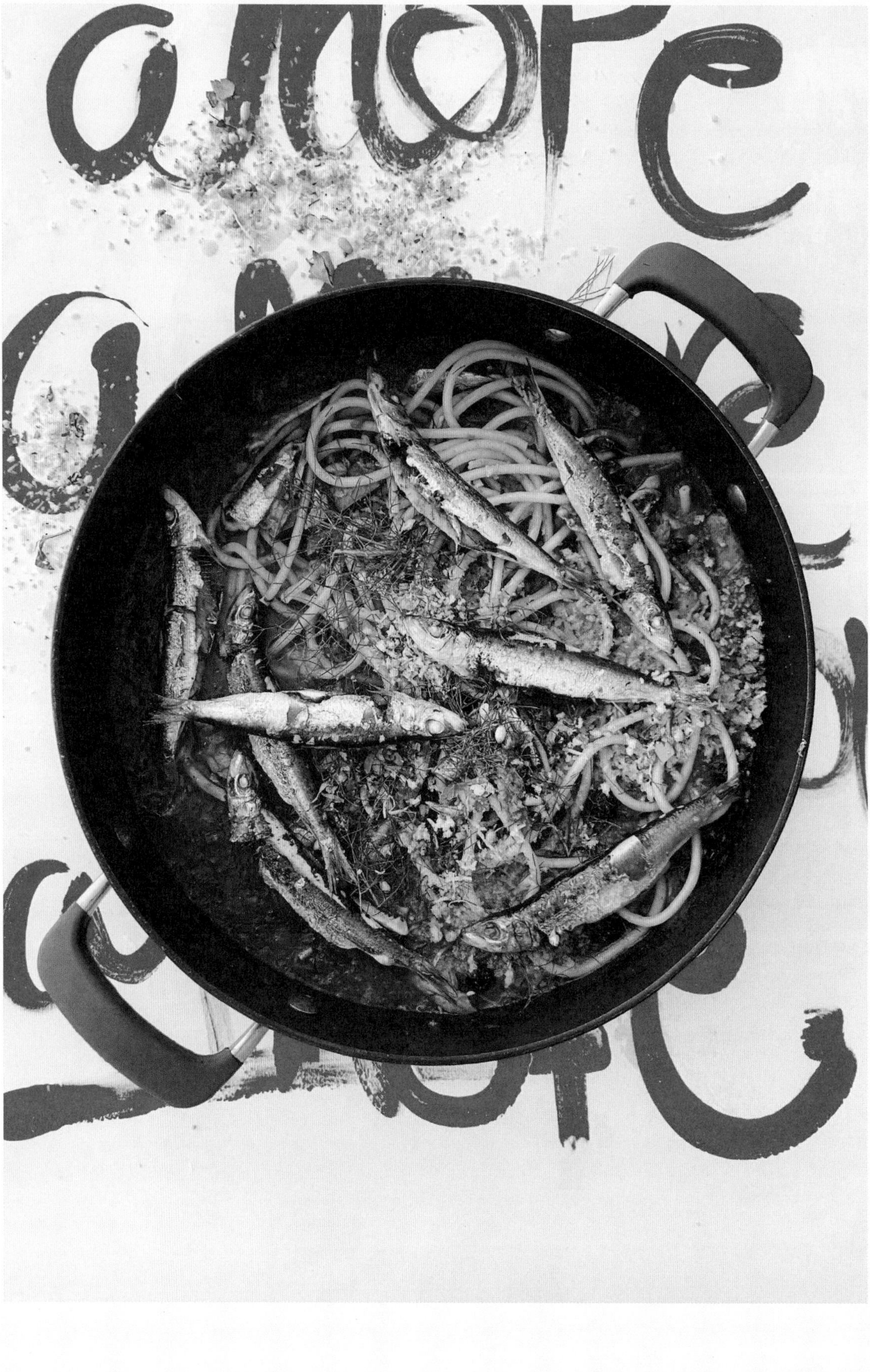
amore

pasta cu li sarde | pasta with sardines

400 g (14 oz) fresh sardines, 8 left whole and
the remaining deboned

2 tablespoons mild olive oil, plus 1 tablespoon
extra for frying the sardines

1 small brown onion, diced

2 garlic cloves, crushed

60 g (2 oz/1 cup) wild fennel fronds or dill,
roughly chopped, plus extra to serve

1 heaped tablespoon tomato paste
(concentrated puree)

60 g (2 oz/½ cup) raisins, currants or sultanas

125 ml (4 fl oz/½ cup) dry white wine

400 g (14 oz) tinned chopped tomatoes

400 g (14 oz) bucatini

salt and freshly ground black pepper

80 g (2¾ oz/½ cup) lightly toasted pine nuts, to serve

chopped flat-leaf (Italian) parsley, to serve

Pangrattato (page 26), to serve

enough for 4–6

If you need to debone the sardines, begin by removing the heads. Run your thumb down the belly
of the sardine towards the tail, removing the innards as you go. Remove the fins and all the spiny
bits. Open the sardine up and pull one side of the sardine away from the backbone. Set aside.
Grab the tail and pull away the backbone from the other side. Rinse the sardines under cold
running water and set aside.

To make the sauce, heat the oil in a large frying pan over a medium heat, then gently fry the
onions until soft, about 5 minutes. Add the garlic, fennel, tomato paste, raisins and wine and cook
on a medium–high heat until the wine has reduced by half, around 5 minutes. Season with salt
and pepper. Add the tomatoes and cook for another 10 minutes. Add all of the deboned sardines
to the pan and simmer until they are cooked, around 5 minutes.

Meanwhile, bring a large saucepan of water to the boil, add salt and cook the bucatini until
al dente. Drain and combine the pasta with the sardine sauce, gently tossing.

While the pasta is cooking, fry the eight whole sardines. Heat the extra olive oil in a large frying
pan on a low heat and gently fry the sardines for about 2–3 minutes on each side.

Serve the pasta in individual bowls, then top with a sprinkle of pine nuts, some chopped dill and
parsley and a tablespoon or two of *pangrattato*. Top with one or two of the fried sardines.

———

Pasta cu li sarde could almost be called the national dish of Sicily, especially in the western
provinces around Palermo. The richest interpretation includes saffron, raisins, pine nuts, fresh
sardines, wild fennel and is illuminated by a golden crown of *pangrattato*. Nonna Giuseppa
wrapped bundles of fennel tightly with kitchen twine before simmering in her sauce to intensify
the flavour, removing it just before serving. If you like, in place of the wild fennel or dill, you can
use the fronds and stems from 1 fennel bulb. Use the bulb for a salad.

maccarruni with napoli

Fresh tomato sauce 1 (page 30)

Flour and water dough (page 34)

semolina flour, for dusting

1 *buso* or very long bamboo skewer

freshly grated pecorino, to serve

enough for 4–6

Make the fresh tomato sauce as instructed. Follow the recipe for making the pasta dough on page 34.

Cut the dough into four portions and cover with a tea towel to stop a dry crust from forming.

Get comfortable – the next step may take an hour (or 30 minutes with two people). Prepare your work surface with a clean area for rolling dough into ropes and an area dusted with semolina flour, just above to the right or left, for flicking the maccarruni once they are twisted.

Take one portion (at a time) of the dough and break it off into a piece about the size of a small walnut. Roll it into a long rope, roughly about 50 cm (19¾ in) long. Cut this into three portions. Take one little rope and place it on the end of a *buso* or skewer. Pinch it down to grip the end of the skewer. Under the palms of both hands roll backwards and forwards to twist the rope around the skewer. Gently slide the maccarruni off the skewer, flick it onto the floured surface and dust with semolina. There's no need to cover them at this stage. Repeat this step until all the dough has been rolled and twirled into maccarruni.

Bring a large saucepan of water to the boil, add salt and cook the maccarruni until al dente. Drain and combine the pasta with the warm sauce, gently tossing.

Serve with freshly grated pecorino.

—

If you're not in the mood for a classic tomato sauce, you can choose any one of the pesto-style sauces on page 33 to serve with the maccarruni.

maccarruni alla trapanese

300 g (10½ oz) dried maccheroni al ferretto pasta or 300 g (10½ oz) homemade maccarruni pasta (page 48)

Trapanese pesto (page 33)

155 g (5½ oz/1 cup) whole toasted almonds, roughly chopped, plus extra to serve

freshly grated pecorino, to serve

extra-virgin olive oil, to serve

freshly ground black pepper, to serve

1 lemon, cut into wedges, to serve

enough for 4

Bring a large saucepan of water to the boil, add salt and cook the pasta until al dente. Drain the pasta, leaving some pasta water clinging to the maccarruni. Return the pasta to the saucepan and gently stir through the pesto and almonds.

Serve on individual plates with grated pecorino, extra almonds, a drizzle of extra-virgin olive oil and a little black pepper. Place a wedge or two of lemon on the side.

—

Sicilian cooking and summer are made for each other. This is the perfect recipe for a slippery, lazy afternoon of eating and resting in the soft, gossamer-warm-thin rhythms of summer. This dish has so few ingredients. The secret to this recipe is to use the ripest tomatoes you can find.

gnocchi with roasted tomatoes

freshly grated pecorino or ricotta salata, to serve

roasted tomato sauce

125 ml (4 fl oz/½ cup) mild olive oil

60 g (2 oz) salted butter, chopped

1 kg (2 lb 3 oz) very ripe tomatoes,
a mix of large and cherry

7 garlic cloves, skins on

handful thyme sprigs

3 tablespoons vincotto

1 teaspoon white (granulated) sugar

salt and freshly ground black pepper

gnocchi

1.3 kg (2 lb 14 oz) peeled and halved boiling
potatoes, such as desiree, skin on

150 g (5½ oz/1 cup) tipo 00 flour, sifted,
plus extra for dusting

pinch of salt

pinch of nutmeg

enough for 8

Preheat the oven to 200°C (390°F).

To make the roasted tomato sauce, pour the olive oil into an ovenproof dish, then add the remaining ingredients. Jiggle the pan to coat the ingredients well. Roast, uncovered, for 15 minutes. Remove the dish from the oven and gently press the mixture with a potato masher. Continue to roast for another 15 minutes, or until the tomatoes are all squishy and bubbly in a pool of juice. Check the seasoning, set aside and keep warm.

To make the gnocchi, cook the potatoes in a large pot of cold salted water, bring to the boil, then simmer until tender but not falling apart, around 20–30 minutes. Meanwhile, combine the flour, a good pinch of salt and nutmeg in a large bowl and set aside. Drain the potatoes and allow them to cool for a little, then peel. Pass them through a food mill or potato ricer (if using a potato masher, mash as smooth as possible, making sure there are no lumps) directly into the flour mixture. Starting under the flour, use your hands to turn this into the potatoes until the mixture comes together as a dough. It will look a little rough – try not to overwork the dough or the gnocchi will end up tough.

Pinch off a portion of the dough and, on a lightly floured surface, start rolling it into a rope shape, 1.5 cm (½ in) in diameter. Cut it into 2.5 cm (1 in) lengths. Cook batches of gnocchi in salted, gently boiling water until they tumble freely on the surface, about 1–2 minutes. Once they come to the surface, leave them to cook for another minute. Remove from the water with a slotted spoon and place directly into the dish with the tomato sauce, gently jiggling the pan. Set aside and keep warm until all the gnocchi are cooked and ready to serve at the table for your guests to help themselves. Don't forget a big bowl of freshly grated pecorino for people to add their own cheese.

—

My grandbabies' favourite dish is any pasta with lovely green pesto. Especially Theodore (Teddy), who is a natural at making gnocchi. All my grandbabies love potatoes, particularly when made into gnocchi. They become lost in a stream of silence until they all ask for 'More please Nonno'. There is no more precious moment than this.

spaghetti with raw tomatoes | This spaghetti has a unique, pungent, raw garlic flavour
that is almost spicy, which pairs with the squishy, acidic zing of fresh raw tomatoes and basil.
Prepare a batch of Raw tomato sauce (page 31). Bring a large saucepan of water to the boil,
add salt and cook 500 g (1 lb 2 oz) spaghetti until al dente. Before draining the spaghetti,
reserve 125 ml (4 fl oz/½ cup) pasta water. Return the drained spaghetti to the pan, pour in the
pasta water and combine with the raw tomato sauce, gently tossing. Serve on individual plates
and sprinkle with ricotta salata. As an alternative, when making the sauce use flat-leaf (Italian)
parsley instead of basil and more garlic. Enough for 4–6.

penne lisce alla norma | Prepare a batch of Fresh tomato sauce 2 (page 30). Preheat the oven to 200°C (390°F). Line a baking tray with baking paper and brush it with olive oil. Put 1 eggplant (aubergine), chopped into finger-size chips, into a bowl, drizzle with a little mild olive oil and season with salt. Mix to thoroughly coat the eggplant, then spread it out on the prepared tray. Roast until lightly golden brown, about 20–30 minutes, then set aside. Bring a large saucepan of water to the boil, add salt and cook 500 g (1 lb 2 oz) penne until al dente. Drain the pasta and return it to the pan, add the tomato sauce and gently toss. Serve on individual plates topped with the eggplant and sprinkle with freshly grated ricotta salata. Enough for 4–6.

linguine, pancetta and anchovies

80 ml (2½ fl oz/⅓ cup) mild olive oil

6 slices pancetta, finely chopped

1 small brown onion, finely chopped

1 garlic clove, finely chopped

2 bird's eye chillies, finely chopped

16 cherry tomatoes, halved

small bunch of wild fennel fronds or dill including stems and leaves, very tightly wrapped in kitchen twine

250 g (9 oz) white anchovies

60 g (2 oz) baby capers

1 tablespoon red-wine vinegar

small handful flat-leaf (Italian) parsley, finely chopped

500 g (1 lb 2 oz) linguine

salt and freshly ground black pepper

enough for 4–6

Heat the oil in a large frying pan over a medium heat, then gently fry the pancetta until crisp, about 7–8 minutes. Put a little of the fried pancetta aside for serving, then add the onion to the pan and fry until translucent, about 5 minutes. Add the garlic, chilli, cherry tomatoes, fennel and season with salt and pepper. Gently fry for another 10 minutes, or until the tomatoes have softened a little (but not too squishy).

Take the pan off the heat and add the anchovies, capers, vinegar and parsley and stir. Discard the fennel.

Bring a large saucepan of water to the boil, add salt and cook the linguine until al dente. Before draining, reserve 125 ml (4 fl oz/½ cup) of the pasta water. Drain the pasta, leaving some pasta water clinging to the linguine. Return the linguine to the saucepan, pour in the reserved pasta water and gently stir through the sauce. Serve on individual plates and top with the reserved crisp pancetta.

—

A quick satisfying dish made with white anchovies, crisp pancetta and cherry tomatoes. A few ingredients combine to create a simple, delicious, respectful meal – it's the act of making things beautiful.

When grandbaby number one, Raphael, was four years old, he ordered extra anchovies with his pizza. The moment lingers still and the look with raised eyebrows the Italian waiter gave me. The next time we visit, the same waiter takes our order, announcing with a flourish of hands, pen and paper as he turns to Raphael sand says, 'I remember you – extra anchovies'. Raph with a deadpan face looks up and corrects him, 'That's double anchovies!'

polpette

125 ml (4¼ fl oz/½ cup) extra-virgin olive oil

400 g (14 oz) gnocchetti sardi

freshly grated pecorino, to serve

meatballs

500 g (1 lb 2 oz) premium lean minced (ground) beef

500 g (1 lb 2 oz) premium lean minced (ground) pork

100 g (3½ oz) pecorino, freshly grated

3 garlic cloves, crushed

100 g (3½ oz) Japanese breadcrumbs or 4 slices of fresh white bread processed into breadcrumbs

2 tablespoons finely chopped flat-leaf (Italian) parsley

6 eggs, lightly beaten (I use extra-large eggs for this recipe, around 60 g/2 oz)

salt and freshly ground black pepper

sauce

2 × 400 g (14 oz) tinned finely chopped tomatoes

1 tablespoon white (granulated) sugar

1 good handful of fresh oregano, chopped

salt and freshly ground black pepper

makes 62/enough for 10

To make the meatballs, combine all of the meatball ingredients in a large bowl and season with salt and pepper. Mix well by hand. Add 125 ml (4 fl oz/½ cup) of water and mix again to loosen the mixture a little. Cover the bowl with cling wrap and refrigerate for 2–3 hours for all the flavours to dance and get along with each other. Before you start to form the balls, scoop a tablespoon of the mixture and fry it to check the seasoning. Adjust if required. With damp hands, form the mixture into balls about the size of a table tennis ball. Set aside on an oiled baking tray.

Preheat the oven to 180°C (360°F). Prepare a large roasting tin by brushing half of the olive oil over the base.

Heat the remaining olive oil in a large, deep frying pan over a medium heat, then gently fry half of the polpette, turning them over as they get a little colour. Transfer this batch to the roasting tin and cook for about 15–20 minutes. Set aside and keep warm.

While the first batch of polpette are in the oven, fry the remaining meatballs in the pan, adding a little more oil if required. This time, once the polpette get a little colour, add the tomatoes, 125 ml (4 fl oz/½ cup) water, sugar, oregano and season with salt and pepper, stirring to combine. Bring to the boil, then reduce the heat to low and simmer for 20–30 minutes.

Serve both types of polpette on separate platters for your guests to help themselves. Alternatively, if you have a big enough saucepan you can cook all of the polpette in the sauce (double the sauce ingredients). You could also serve the polpette and sauce with pasta. Once the pasta is cooked, add it to the polpette and sauce and allow it to rest for 2–3 minutes with the lid on. Divide between individual bowls and serve with pecorino.

tomato, cucumber and green olive salad | Combine 4 quartered roma (plum) tomatoes,
4 chopped baby Lebanese (short) cucumbers, 220 g (8 oz/1 cup) pitted, halved green olives,
2 sliced spring onions (scallions), 60 g (2 oz/1 cup) chopped basil leaves, 1 finely sliced red onion
and 1 teaspoon coarsely ground dried fennel seeds in a large bowl and season with salt and
freshly ground black pepper. Drizzle with extra-virgin olive oil and a squeeze of lemon juice.
Mix gently to combine and serve immediately. Enough for 4.

fennel and orange salad | Wash and trim 1 fennel bulb. Usually, store-bought fennel stems are about 10 cm (4 in) long. Keep them with all the furry leaves to add to the salad or use them for soup or seafood dishes. Thinly cut the fennel diagonally starting from the top of the stems. Put the fennel in a large mixing bowl. Dress with the juice of ½ a lemon, then add 30 g (1 oz/1 cup) roughly chopped celery leaves, 1 crushed garlic clove, 1 Lebanese (short) cucumber, halved lengthways and thinly sliced diagonally, and 1 spring onion (scallion), thinly sliced diagonally. Peel, trim and slice 1 orange into discs and add to the bowl, then squeeze any juice from the peel over the top of the salad. Gently toss the salad. Add 80 g (2¾ oz) creamy mascarpone on top and scatter 180 g (6½ oz/1 cup) halved black grapes. Season with salt and freshly ground black pepper. Drizzle with 2 tablespoons extra-virgin olive oil. Enough for 4.

cabbage with peas and casarecce

200 g (7 oz) dried chickpeas, soaked overnight

125 ml (4 fl oz/½ cup) mild olive oil

1 brown onion, finely chopped

1 celery stalk, finely chopped

1 carrot, finely chopped

1 long red chilli, finely chopped

4 garlic cloves, finely chopped

1 teaspoon each of fennel seeds, ground cumin and ground coriander

2 tablespoons tomato paste (concentrated puree)

4 ripe tomatoes, skinned, seeded and chopped or 400 g (14 oz) tinned chopped tomatoes

200 g (7 oz/1⅓ cup) fresh or frozen peas

400 g (14 oz) white cabbage, chopped

300 g (10½ oz) casarecce pasta

salt and freshly ground black pepper

good handful basil leaves and flower heads, to serve

enough for 4–6

Drain the chickpeas and set aside. Heat the oil in a large saucepan over medium heat. Add the onion, celery, carrot, chilli, salt and pepper and gently fry until the onion is soft, about 6–8 minutes. Add the garlic, fennel seeds, cumin, coriander, tomato paste and chickpeas and gently fry for about 1 minute. Add the tomatoes and half of the peas and cabbage. Cover with a lid and cook gently for about 10 minutes, stirring occasionally.

Add 3 litres (101 fl oz) of water, cover again and bring to the boil. Turn the heat down to low–medium and cook for a further 1 hour, partially covered.

Add the casarecce and cook until the pasta is al dente. Five minutes before the pasta is ready, add the reserved peas. Check the seasoning and adjust if necessary. Ladle into serving bowls and scatter with basil.

—

While eating a plate of cabbage with peas and casarecce, grandbaby number three, Otto, said, 'Nonno, you have twenty cats on your head, your bum pops and burbs'. The conversation that followed deteriorated into a mash of words between Otto and Leni only they understood. I positively relish these moments with plenty of giggly and funny noises. All four grandbabies delight in using words and phrases like snot, fart, bum and 'Nonno is a poo-poo head'.

saffron risotto

1 litre (34 fl oz/4 cups) vegetable or chicken stock

3 tablespoons mild olive oil

40 g (1½ oz) salted butter

1 leek, trimmed and finely chopped

½ fennel bulb, trimmed and finely chopped

250 g (9 oz/1 cup) arborio rice

125 ml (4 fl oz/½ cup) dry white wine or marsala

½ teaspoon saffron powder

1 teaspoon smoked paprika

1 tablespoon tomato paste (concentrated puree)

1 bay leaf

3 thyme sprigs, plus extra to serve

3 sage leaves

100 g (3½ oz) shiitake mushrooms, halved

100 g (3½ oz) mild olives

3 tablespoons freshly grated pecorino, plus extra to serve

salt and freshly ground black pepper

enough for 4

Bring the stock to a simmer in a large saucepan. Heat the oil and half the butter in a large heavy-based saucepan over a medium heat. Add the leek, fennel, season with salt and cook, stirring, until the leeks are soft, around 6–8 minutes. Stir in the rice and cook for 2 minutes – you'll hear it toasting – then add the wine and cook, stirring, until it's absorbed. Add the saffron, paprika, tomato paste and cook for a further 2 minutes. Add the bay leaf and herbs, stir, then add 250 ml (8½ fl oz/1 cup) of the simmering stock and stir until absorbed. Keep adding stock gradually in this way for about 10 minutes. Halfway through the last cup of stock stir in the mushrooms and olives.

Remove from the heat and stir in the pecorino and remaining butter. Check the seasoning.

Serve in warm bowls with extra pecorino on top.

—

For centuries, countries sharing the Mediterranean coastline have been criss-crossing and influencing each other with clandestine meetings dressed in gold, orange and red. The King and Queen of spices – saffron and paprika – are that special something that collide to make magical secrets of their own. Raphael, our eldest grandbaby, is an avid reader inspired by the grandeur of the gods of Roman and Greek mythology and is also drawn to many cultures and time periods. His imagination visits the glorious cities of the Roman Empire, whose voices drift in and out of his short-story writing.

chicory and barley risotto

150 g (5½ oz/⅔ cup) white pearl barley

1.5 litres (51 fl oz/6 cups) *Jojo's brodo* (page 21)
 or chicken stock

3 tablespoons mild olive oil

75 g (2¾ oz) salted butter

4 shallots, finely chopped

2 celery stalks, finely chopped

1 small fennel bulb, diced

2 tablespoons tomato paste (concentrated puree)

4 garlic cloves, crushed

pinch of chilli flakes

1 tablespoon fennel seeds, crushed

100 g (3½ oz) field mushrooms, thinly sliced

1 bunch chicory (endive), finely chopped

100 ml (3½ fl oz/⅓ cup) dry marsala

75 g (2¾ oz) pecorino, freshly grated

salt and freshly ground black pepper

100 g (3½ oz) soft goat's cheese, to serve

enough for 4

In a large saucepan, combine the barley with the *brodo* and bring to the boil. Turn the heat down to low and gently simmer until the barley is tender, about 20 minutes. Drain the barley, retaining the *brodo*, and set aside.

Heat the oil and butter in a large heavy-based pan over a medium heat, then add the shallots, celery, fennel and season with salt and pepper. Gently cook until the shallots are soft, around 6–8 minutes. Add the tomato paste, garlic, chilli flakes and fennel seeds and stir for 1 minute. Add the mushrooms and chicory, and cook for another 5 minutes, stirring, until the chicory has wilted. Add the barley and stir through to mix well. Cook for a few minutes, just long enough to warm the barley through. Add the marsala – once the marsala is completely absorbed, add the reserved *brodo* and stir it in, leaving it a little wet. Heat until the *brodo* is hot and ready to serve. Check the seasoning, then add the pecorino and stir it through.

Serve in individual bowls and top with crumbled goat's cheese.

———

My brother Frank and I commenced classes in 1960 at The Immaculate Conception, St Mary's Catholic Primary School in Hastings run by the Sisters of St Joseph. We ate our lunch in the shelter sheds. My lunchbox included fried chicory sandwiches with pecorino cheese in thick-cut pasta dura. Sometimes there were fried red capsicums (bell peppers) with caramelised onions, which I pretended was ham and tomato sauce. Our lunches always smelt like walking into a pizza restaurant: first it was the garlic that hit you, then the capsicum and onions.

Our classroom walls were painted pink, the floor tiles were a grey-and-pink check pattern. The cupboards under the blackboard were coral pink. Sister Agnes, our principal, and the other nuns wore brown – as did Joseph, Jesus's father. The grade five teacher, Sister Xaviour, was just under 5 ft, rotund and jolly. A year after I arrived at Saint Mary's, the nuns thought I had a talent for drawing. They entered my work on the history of the 'Sisters in Australia' into an art book competition. My design was given a high commendation.

chicken alla puttanesca

3 tablespoons mild olive oil

4 × 250 g (9 oz) chicken breasts, skin on

200 g (7 oz) large zucchini, quartered lengthways and cut into thick slices

3 garlic cloves, lightly smashed

3 anchovy fillets (I use the little ones in a jar)

200 g (7 oz) cherry tomatoes, some halved

400 g (14 oz) tinned chopped tomatoes

1 teaspoon white (granulated) sugar

90 g (3 oz/½ cup) black olives, unpitted

2 tablespoons baby capers

chilli flakes, to taste

salt and freshly ground black pepper

90 g (3 oz/⅓ cup) Basil and spinach pesto (page 33), to serve

lemon wedges, to serve

enough for 4

Heat the oil in a heavy-based saucepan over a high heat. Cook the chicken breasts, skin side down, until golden brown, about 5 minutes. Turn the chicken and cook for 3 minutes on a low–medium heat. Remove the chicken from the pan and set aside. In the same pan, cook the marrow over a medium heat until lightly golden on both sides, around 10 minutes. Season with salt and pepper. Remove the marrow and set aside.

Add the garlic and anchovies to the pan and fry over a low–medium heat, stirring, until the garlic is lightly golden. Add all the tomatoes and sugar and raise the heat to medium–high, stirring occasionally until the mixture starts to bubble. Turn the heat down to low, add the chicken, skin side up, and cover with the lid slightly ajar to cook for 10 minutes, or until the chicken is cooked through. Stir in the zucchini, olives, capers and chilli flakes. Remove from the heat, cover with foil to keep warm, rest for 10–15 minutes and serve in individual bowls topped with pesto and a wedge of lemon.

——

Puttanesca only needs a glance from garlic, a touch from anchovy, a smooth voluptuous red glow from ripe tomatoes and a swirling skirt of capers and olives seeping just enough salty tears to embrace you. Beneath its brutal, savoury deliciousness are traces of hot peppery chilli flakes, which on a summer's afternoon will satisfy all your needs.

There's one thing we can all agree on: *sugo alla puttanesca* may have been invented in Naples, but it's their chic Sicilian cousins who know how to set the scene for the dish – a room with subdued lighting, a beautiful table adorned with flowers, some soft, cool French jazz playing in the background, a deeply hued red wine with vibrant fruity tones and the humble, fragrant tapestry of *sugo alla puttanesca*.

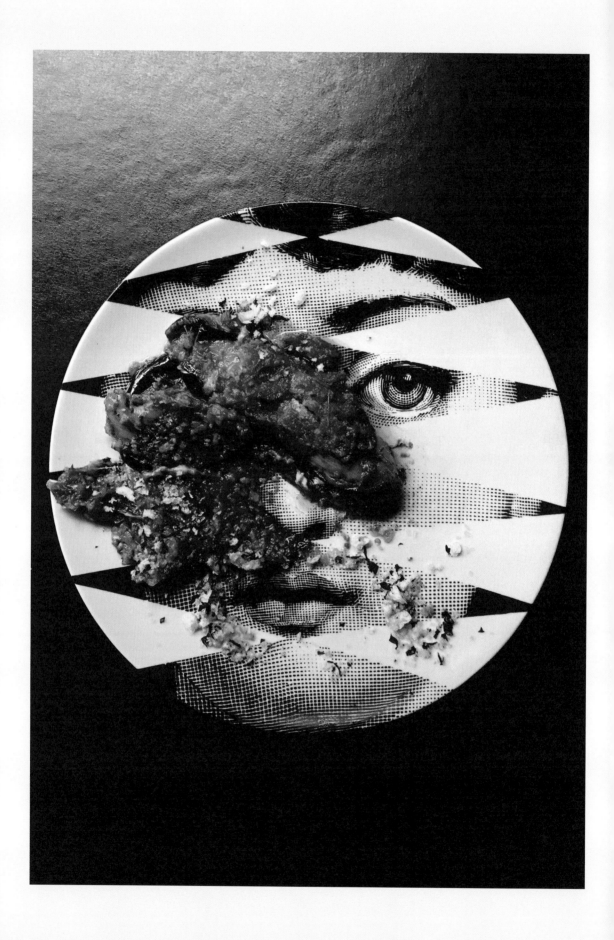

At the top of our giant cypress, a distant grey band of sea with its intricate pattern of civilisation is whirling at the edge of Cumbrae Farm, just like the Strait of Sicily between Tunisia and Malta. Decades later, all four of my grandbabies appear as crowned centaur-like, fantastic creatures from ancient Greek mythology, scattering legends around them in golden flecks of green bonfire. A mammoth, oval raven's nest is wedged towards the top of the cypress with carefully embroidered broken sticks and wire, accessorised with jewels of light, like spirits adrift on old memorial cards of Ferruzzi's *Madonnina*, who has moved into the house below its limbs.

Eavesdropping over brightly patterned walls, I hear droning voices, rifling through prayer books and quickly scattered Hail Marys. Marble-spotted lino and a jumble of polished credenzas are guarded by the elegant shadows of multi-branched chandeliers and towering candelabras.

eggplant parmigiana | Prepare a batch of Fresh tomato sauce 2 or Tinned tomato sauce (page 30). Slice and lightly salt both sides of 3 large eggplants (aubergines). Lay them between paper towel to release their water. Set aside for 30 minutes. Preheat the oven to 200°C (390°F) and brush a baking tray with 2–3 tablespoons mild olive oil. Arrange the eggplant slices on the baking tray. Roast until lightly golden brown on both sides, about 20–30 minutes. Remove them from the oven and reduce the oven temperature to 180°C (360°F). Meanwhile, heat 3 tablespoons mild olive oil in a large frying pan over low heat and gently fry 10 finely chopped shallots until translucent, about 8–10 minutes. Add 120 g (4½ oz/2 cups) Japanese breadcrumbs and fry, stirring constantly, for about 4–5 minutes, until they start to toast to a golden colour. Grate 200 g (7 oz) Parmigiano Reggiano and set aside. Brush a deep, 26 cm (10¼ in) round stoneware dish with oil. Spread a ladleful of sauce, then a layer of eggplant slices into the prepared dish. Add a layer of breadcrumbs, a sprinkle of grated Parmigiano Reggiano, then cover with more sauce. Repeat the layers as before, finishing with sauce and Parmigiano Reggiano. Cook in the oven for 45–60 minutes, until golden. Rest for 15 minutes and garnish with *Pangrattato* (page 26) before serving. Enough for 8.

In summer, the grapevines and roses flourished, twisting and unfolding their way up the pergola connecting our new house to the remnants of the McKirdy's home. The garden was an uproar of colour with ribbon borders of blood-red gladioli alongside Nonna Giuseppa's favourites: lemon verbena, Sweet William, Italian lavender and her beloved Rosa 'Alba Suaveolens', made sweeter by its orange buds unfurling into a jumble of messy yellow and apricot petals. Like in the garden on their farm back in Sicily, they grew purple artichokes with prickly tips whose stems Nonna trimmed, peeled, blanched, then dipped in a garlicky batter and fried until golden.

Eggplants (aubergines), zucchini (courgette) and olives were bottled and stored in the sheds. Garlic was pulled from the ground with stalks, then plaited and hung near the back door for good luck by the true believers whose protection against the archaic language of spells helped alleviate any concerns of vulgar shadows. The garden gave them enough grapes to make their own wine, and onions and green tomatoes were bottled and sheltered in the sheds.

gyotta chiotta giotta

500 g (1 lb 2 oz) *cucuzza longa* (squash),
  peeled and seeded

80 ml (2½ fl oz/⅓ cup) extra-virgin olive oil,
  plus extra to drizzle

155 g (5½ oz/1 cup) shallots, chopped

1 celery stalk, including leaves, chopped

4 garlic cloves, crushed

1 carrot, chopped

¼ teaspoon chilli flakes

500 g (1 lb 2 oz) boiling potatoes,
  peeled and chopped

300 g (10½ oz) white cabbage, shredded

1 kg (2 lb 3 oz) very ripe fresh tomatoes,
  stem ends cut off and flesh grated with
  a box grater into a bowl

30 g (1 oz/1 cup) basil leaves

4 eggs

salt and freshly ground black pepper

freshly grated Parmigiano Reggiano, to serve

crusty bread, to serve

enough for 6–8

Cut the *cucuzza* into three or four tubes. Peel off the exterior pale green skin, then slice the flesh away from the inner seed pulp. Chop into chunks and set aside.

Heat the oil in a heavy-based cast-iron pot over a medium heat, then add the shallots, celery, garlic, carrot, chilli flakes, season with salt and pepper and cook until the shallots are soft, around 6–8 minutes. Add the potatoes, *cucuzza* and cabbage and stir continuously for 2 minutes, so that the vegetables get introduced to the sofrito. Add the tomatoes, basil (more if you like – it's beautiful in this dish) and 1.5 litres (51 fl oz/6 cups) of water and bring to the boil. Turn the heat down to low and simmer for 45 minutes with the lid ajar, or until the vegetables are tender.

When you're just about ready to serve, poach the eggs in the gyotta. Divide the gyotta and eggs between the serving bowls, drizzle with a little extra-virgin olive oil, sprinkle with freshly grated Parmigiano Reggiano and some freshly ground black pepper. Serve with crusty bread to dunk in the broth.

—

Gyotta, chiotta or giotta – however you spell it, it's a Sicilian summer soup. *Cucuzza longa* are like zucchini (courgette) – if you take your eyes off them they can double in size overnight. Unlike zucchini, they can grow up to 1 m (39 in) long. The tender shoots or curly young tendrils (*tenerumi*), loved by Sicilians, are picked young and dropped into soups. You can make a green version of this soup using the *tenerumi* without the tomatoes. Add the *tenerumi* and broken vermicelli or angel hair pasta to boiling salted water and cook until the pasta is al dente. Divide between bowls and drizzle with extra-virgin olive oil.

My most memorable childhood experiences came from Sunday lunches at Cumbrae. In summer we ate *cucuzza longa* (squash) in so many different ways: in light summer soups, fried with broken eggs, caramelised onions, cherry tomatoes and red capsicum, or cut into large chunks and served in a simple *brodo* (broth) with potatoes and garden snails.

I fell in love with Cumbrae from the very first morning. I'd wake up in the countryside to disappear for the rest of the day; finding beauty in so many things. It was this exploration, and the food we ate, that empowered me to express myself creatively.

We made our own cheese from Mary the Jersey cow and cared for the chooks, young calves and pigs on the farm with a tenderness that was incongruous with the complexity of their disappearance in our young lives. It is odd how we faced this hand-to-mouth experience, to live through the seasons, especially summer, which never failed to surprise with its warm bay-swept wind dancing through a fanfare of long grass and the shadows of ancestors who had long lived and loved this country.

I still dream of that place, regularly reminiscing about it to the woman I love. Jojo's simple plate of fresh, grilled *cucuzza* is one of the warmest culinary memories of all.

grilled cucuzza | This is Jojo's recipe for grilling my brother Frank's *cucuzza longa* (squash). A good Sicilian or Italian greengrocer (or neighbour) should have these for sale or growing in the backyard. Cut *cucuzza* into 1 cm (½ in) thick slices, brush with mild olive oil and season with salt and pepper. Use a barbecue or chargrill pan to grill over a medium–high heat until charred on both sides. Instead of *cucuzza* try this recipe with zucchini (courgette) or a small marrow.

Christmas, Easter, birthdays and picnics were large family
gatherings. Early on 24 December 1959, Dad and Nonno Gaetano
bought eight live, plump birds from the Victoria Market. That
was the first time I saw Nonno and Dad killing chooks. In the
afternoon, Nonna Giuseppa and Mum started making *brodo*
with two of the birds, the rest were for roasting. When aunts
and uncles arrived, everyone began to make little tortelloni to
have with the *brodo*. The pillows were the size of walnuts and
filled with the minced (ground) *brodo* chicken and mixed with
just-cooked minced pork neck, finely chopped mortadella, ricotta,
egg yolk, Parmigiano Reggiano and a pinch of nutmeg.

On Christmas Day large dishes of antipasti were
served with mortadella, salami, provolone and olives. There were
bowls of golden arancini the size of oranges and ricotta-filled
cannoli, *cotoletta* (crumbed veal cutlet), rabbit ragu and dishes
of barbecued squid and fish brushed with herbs, garlic and
lemon. Everyone brought their own version of *cuddureddi*
(Christmas cookies) and crostoli. Watermelon was kept cool in
a bathtub full of cold water. And there was the first of summer's
sun-dried tomatoes.

semi-dried tomatoes | Jars of these semi-dried (sun-blushed) tomatoes make terrific gifts,
especially when adorned with string tied around a little twig of bay leaves. Cut 3 kg (6 lb 10 oz)
roma (plum) tomatoes lengthways and lay them cut side up on a wire rack over a baking tray.
Sprinkle with a little salt and cover with mesh. Allow to dry over 3 or 4 very hot summer days,
turning after 1 day. Alternatively, slowly roast the tomatoes in a preheated 130°C (265°F) oven
for about 2–3 hours. Store in sterilised glass jars with extra-virgin olive oil, chopped garlic,
parsley and freshly ground black pepper. Makes 450–500 g (1 lb–1 lb 2 oz).

grilled prawns | There is nothing more delicious than eating aromatic barbecued prawns (shrimp) with your fingers. Starting with 24 prawns, butterfly some of the prawns by laying them on their backs and, with kitchen scissors or a sharp serrated knife, cut through lengthways from the tails right through to the heads (keep the heads on). Put the butterflied prawns in a large bowl with the unshelled prawns. Add 3 tablespoons extra-virgin olive oil, 1–2 teaspoons chilli flakes (to taste), 3 sliced garlic cloves, the grated zest and juice of 1 lemon and season with salt and freshly ground black pepper. Combine well to coat the prawns. Heat a barbecue grill and cook the prawns for 3–4 minutes, or until they start to turn pink. Take off the heat. Toss into a serving dish with 15 g (½ oz/½ cup) each of finely chopped parsley and mint, and 1 lemon cut into wedges. Enough for 4.

orange coconut cake

450 g (1 lb/3 cups) plain (all-purpose) flour, sifted

3 teaspoons baking powder, sifted

345 g (12 oz/1½ cups) caster sugar

4 eggs

250 ml (8½ fl oz/1 cup) sunflower oil

1 tablespoon limoncello

1 teaspoon natural vanilla extract

250 g (9 oz/1 cup) mascarpone, at room temperature

grated zest and juice of 1 orange

icing

250 g (9 oz/2 cups) icing (confectioners') sugar, sifted

3 tablespoons mascarpone, at room temperature

2 tablespoons orange juice

100 g (3½ oz) coconut flakes, toasted

enough for 8–10

Preheat the oven to 180°C (360°F). Grease a 22 cm (8¾ in) angel food cake tin with butter and line the centre tube with baking paper.

Combine the flour, baking powder and caster sugar in a large bowl and mix well.

In another bowl, combine the eggs, oil, limoncello, vanilla and mix well with a balloon whisk. Whisk in the mascarpone, orange zest and juice until well combined. Add the wet mixture to the dry and fold it through with a spatula until just incorporated.

Spoon the batter into the prepared tin and bake for 50 minutes, or until it tests done with a skewer. Remove from the oven and leave to cool in the tin completely. Once cool, gently turn the cake out onto a wire rack positioned over a baking tray.

To prepare the icing (frosting), whisk together the icing sugar, mascarpone and orange juice until smooth. Pour the icing over the top and side of the cake – the baking tray will catch any drips. Transfer to a large plate and top with the toasted coconut.

This cake is best served straight away or the same day, but it will keep for up to 2 days stored in an airtight container in the refrigerator (bring to room temperature before serving).

—

I find inspiration for cooking everywhere – art history and books on design, especially fashion. The men in my family, especially my father and my father-in-law, Vincenzo, dressed like movie stars with crisp, white shirts and beautifully tailored suits with big lapels and patterned ties. My mother has what I call a very autobiographical style and a confidence in whatever she wears. At primary school the nuns wore chocolate brown in winter and pure, crisp, flowing whites in summer, while the priests were draped in brilliant scarlet and shiny gold. Sister Francis – whose classes were a complete joy – loved art, especially the paintings of English rococo artist Thomas Gainsborough. His painting of Mary Countess Howe draped in clouds of pink silk, five rows of pearls around her neck and wearing an Italian straw hat reminds me of the priests' robes. The exaggerated ruffled sleeves and lace pinafore showcase intricate layering, pleating and feathering of cloth. Everything resonates with the natural world behind her. Countess Howe's gown inspired the simplicity for the icing on the cake in this recipe, replicating the rows of pearls worn around her neck.

At Cumbrae Farm there were two Clydesdales: a black, burly able-bodied horse who loved running in the opposite direction whenever we came near, and a small, older bay with white spots on its belly. Both had gorgeous white feathery hooves.

My parents purchased Cumbrae with the Russo brothers, Uncle Joe and Uncle Jack, who arrived in Australia from Alicudi (in the Aeolian Islands off Sicily) in the late 1940s. Joe and Jack tended their area of land at weekends.

A handful of sheds, including the stables for the horses, were full of stuff: wood piles of dependable timber, rusted metal gates, weathered wooden ladders, crusty corrugated sheets, worn out brooms, concrete troughs, piles of dusty hessian sacks and old fruit boxes. These sheds held a country cornucopia of faded natural wonders. There were baskets brimming with all sorts of history talking through children's writing on faded grey-rendered walls. In dark corners, the shilly-shallying of shadows cast a vertical cinema of life-size galloping horses, monkeys and birds sipping Darjeeling from gold-rimmed Italian coffee cups painted cerulean blue, lemon yellow and red.

Some of the timber from the sheds was used to build our new home behind the existing house, which was eventually knocked down.

In one shed Dad found an old box gramophone under
a stack of rusted machinery. In another corner of the shed
stood a Victorian washing machine with wooden ringers and a
big wheel handle in letter-box red – after a scrub it was in good
working order. There were old washboards and tubs everywhere.
Everything was covered in thick layers of grey dust and cobwebs.
Dad wondered if the old 'talking machine' could play his 78 rpm
vinyl records. He loved operas and musicals, especially his
beloved *Oklahoma*. Whenever I hear Rodgers and Hammerstein's
'Oh, what a beautiful morning', it always reminds me of him.

These sheds held generations of *histoire de la curiosité*,
which had, over time, acquired beauty, character and charm.
I've always had this excessive book-buying thing. I'm sure it's
a vice that started to germinate in those sheds stacked to the
rafters. In nearly every house I've lived in there have been shelves
of books kept in no particular order except for cooking, art and
design sharing some commonality. For decades, the solitary
confinement of these spaces became the art and life of comfort
– just enough away from the outside world. The tranquillity and
stillness suited me; its meditative intensity feeding a perfectionist
vision of the work to come. Loving nothing better than running
in the opposite direction.

pear pudding

5 william (bartlett) pears, halved with stems and pips (optional) included

250 ml (8½ fl oz/1 cup) Alchermes liqueur

80 g (2¾ oz/⅓ cup) soft brown sugar

4 cloves

4 star anise

5 croissants, torn into pieces, some big, some small

2 pinches of freshly ground nutmeg

2 pinches of ground cinnamon

6 eggs

60 g (2 oz/½ cup) icing (confectioners') sugar

375 ml (12½ fl oz/1½ cups) thick (double/heavy) cream

375 ml (12½ fl oz/1½ cups) buttermilk

grated zest of 1 orange

yoghurt, ice-cream or thick (double/heavy) cream, to serve

almond crystals

60 g (2 oz/¼ cup) caster sugar

2 tablespoons maple syrup

100 g (3½ oz) flaked almonds

enough for 8

Preheat the oven to 180°C (360°F). Line a 22 × 26 cm (8¾ × 10¼ in) roasting tin and a baking tray with baking paper.

Place the pears – with some of them cut side up – in the roasting tin with the Alchermes, brown sugar, cloves and star anise. Cover tightly with foil, then bake for 25–30 minutes. Remove the pears from the oven and take out the cloves and star anise. Place the torn croissants around the pears, pushing the pear halves to stand up with their stems upright. Sprinkle the nutmeg and cinnamon over the top. Set aside.

In a large bowl, combine the eggs, icing sugar, cream, buttermilk and orange zest, whisking by hand. Pour the batter into the tin around the pears. Bake for about 45 minutes, or until the top is golden brown and the custard is firm on the outside but gooey in the middle.

Meanwhile, to make the almond crystals, stir the caster sugar, maple syrup, almonds and 2 tablespoons of water in a small saucepan over low heat until the mixture is clear. When the almond mixture is ready, pour it onto the prepared baking tray. Toast in the oven for about 10 minutes, stirring every now and again to form dry crystals. Cool on the tray.

Remove the pudding from the oven and spoon straight into bowls. Top with the almond crystals and serve immediately with yoghurt, ice-cream or thick cream.

—

Although the croissants are broken, they are somehow more beautiful once cooked. When Jojo and I travel, we always start off walking down the same road. Sometimes I go off onto side streets to explore, while she quietly keeps walking, stopping occasionally to sit at a cafe, watch people or read a book, a finger to her lips, her eyes only lifting to see where I am. I'm always just to her side.

passionfruit and coconut cake

icing (confectioners') sugar, for dusting

cherries, stems attached, to serve

pastry

125 g (4½ oz) unsalted butter, chopped

115 g (4 oz/½ cup) caster sugar

1 egg

pinch of salt

1 teaspoon natural vanilla extract

225 g (8 oz/1½ cups) plain (all-purpose) flour, sifted

1 teaspoon baking powder

35 g (1¼ oz/⅓ cup) almond flour

filling

4 eggs

pinch of salt

115 g (4 oz/½ cup) caster sugar

55 g (2 oz/1 cup) desiccated (shredded) coconut

75 g (2¾ oz/½ cup) plain flour, sifted

375 ml (12½ fl oz/1½ cups) thick (double/heavy) cream, plus extra to serve

160 ml (5½ fl oz/⅔ cup) coconut cream

grated zest and juice of 1 lime

8 passionfruit

enough for 8

Preheat the oven to 180°C (360°F). Grease a 24 cm (9½ in) round cake tin with butter and line with baking paper.

To make the pastry, beat the butter and caster sugar in the bowl of an electric mixer until pale and creamy. Add the egg, salt and vanilla extract and beat until combined. Add the plain flour, baking powder and almond flour and fold until just combined – it will look a bit shaggy. Place the dough into the prepared tin and press down gently to spread it evenly over the base and a little way up the side. Bake for 20 minutes, until it is lightly golden.

Meanwhile, to make the filling, beat the eggs, salt and caster sugar in the bowl of an electric mixer for about 7 minutes, until pale and foamy. Add the coconut, plain flour, thick cream, coconut cream, lime zest and juice and the pulp from four of the passionfruit. Fold gently to combine.

Pour the filling into the pastry case in the tin. Bake for about 1 hour, or until golden brown. Remove the cake from the oven and allow it to cool completely before removing it from the tin.

To serve, place the cake on a serving dish and dust with icing sugar. Serve with the remaining passionfruit cut into halves, along with some fresh cherries and extra thick cream.

This cake will keep for up to 4 days stored in an airtight container in the refrigerator (bring to room temperature before serving).

———

During the writing of this book, Bill Granger, one of my favourite Australian cooks, passed away. I never met Bill but whenever I was in Sydney I would always go to Bill's for breakfast. The first time I made Bill's coconut and passionfruit slice, I misread the method thinking it was a cake. It worked well as a cake – everyone loved it – so it has remained that way ever since.

Being asked to make dessert for Danielle and Donna's Lunar New Year lunch celebration was a wonderful opportunity to bring Chinese, Sicilian and Australian cultures together. Trifle is my favourite dessert ... no wait ... cannoli is ... hang on ... forget the cannoli. We're talking about trifle: elegant, delicate, robust and wonderfully comforting all in one mouthful.

If making your own custard is a little too challenging, it's perfectly fine to use the store-bought variety – yet there is something quite satisfying when making your own. I do urge you to make it yourself, there is no crème more satisfying than custard.

lunar new year trifle

125 ml (4 fl oz/½ cup) dry marsala

125 g (4½ oz) blackberries, cut in half lengthways

300 ml (10 fl oz/1¼ cups) thick (double/heavy) cream

2 dragon fruit, cut into wedges, to serve

extra cream, to serve

jelly

6 gelatine leaves, clear and unflavoured

150 g (5½ oz/⅔ cups) caster sugar

500 g (1 lb 2 oz) small strawberries, halved lengthways

juice of 1 orange

juice of 1 lime

250 g (9 oz) raspberries

sponge cake

4 eggs, at room temperature

145 g (5 oz/⅔ cup) caster sugar

150 g (5½ oz/1 cup) self-raising flour

150 g (5½ oz/1 cup) cornflour (cornstarch)

custard

1 litre (34 fl oz/4 cups) full-cream (whole) milk

4 egg yolks

80 g (2¾ oz/⅓ cup) caster sugar

50 g (1¾ oz) cornflour (cornstarch)

rind of 1 lemon, cut into strips

1 vanilla bean, split lengthways and seeds scraped

1 walnut-size piece of peeled ginger

enough for 8–10

Before you begin, choose your trifle bowl. Mine is 18 cm (7 in) at the base, then tapers out to 21 cm (8¼ in) at the top.

To make the jelly, put the gelatine leaves in a shallow dish with enough cold water to cover them. Leave them to soak for 5–10 minutes, or until soft. Meanwhile, prepare the strawberries. Pour 500 ml (17 fl oz/2 cups) of water into a large saucepan. Add the caster sugar and heat gently over a medium heat, stirring occasionally until the sugar has dissolved, then add the strawberries. Bring to the boil, then turn the heat down so the mixture is barely simmering, and cook for 5 minutes more. Take off the heat. Carefully pour the strawberry mixture through a sieve set over a large heatproof measuring cup (set aside the cooked strawberries). Stir the orange and lime juice into the liquid. You should have about 600 ml (21 fl oz) of liquid. Gently squeeze the excess water from the gelatine leaves before adding them to the strawberry water. Stir well until completely dissolved. Let the liquid cool for about 15 minutes before pouring it into your trifle bowl. Add the cooked strawberries to the trifle bowl and all of the raspberries. Once cold, cover the bowl with cling wrap and refrigerate overnight to set.

To make the sponge cake, preheat the oven to 180°C (360°F). Grease one 16 cm (6¼ in) and one 19 cm (7½ in) round cake tin with butter and line the base and side with baking paper. Beat the eggs and sugar in the bowl of an electric mixer on medium–high for 7 minutes. Meanwhile, sift the flour and cornflour together three times to aerate. Sprinkle the flour over the egg mixture while gently folding it in with a large metal spoon until just combined. Pour the batter into the prepared tins and bake for 15–20 minutes, or until it tests done with a skewer. Cool in the tins for 15 minutes before inverting onto a wire rack and gently peeling away the paper. Leave to cool.

To make the custard, warm the milk in a saucepan over a low heat almost to boiling point, then set aside. Whisk the egg yolks, caster sugar and cornflour together briskly in a large mixing bowl until well combined – the texture should be like smooth ricotta. Gradually pour the milk through a fine-mesh sieve into the egg mixture, whisking constantly. Wipe out the saucepan and pour the mixture back into it. Add the lemon, vanilla bean and ginger and warm over a low heat, stirring intermittently with a balloon whisk, until it thickens, about 20 minutes. Scrape down the side of the pan as you go. Pour through the clean fine-mesh sieve into a bowl and set aside.

To assemble the trifle, place the small sponge cake on top of the strawberry and raspberry jelly in the trifle bowl. Lightly brush the sponge cake with marsala. Place the blackberry halves, stem side down, around the sponge cake with the cut side showing through the glass. The berries should be almost level with the top of the sponge cake. Now pour in some of the custard (keep the rest for serving). It will trickle down between the berries. Top with the larger sponge cake, gently positioning it in the centre of the bowl and pushing down slightly – this will spread the custard out a little to reach the glass. Lightly brush the top of the sponge cake with the remaining marsala. Cover with cling wrap and refrigerate overnight. When ready to serve, spread the thick cream over the top, right to the edges, and top with the dragon fruit. Serve with a little of the leftover custard. Extra cream won't hurt either.

———

Start the process of making the trifle two days ahead. Each layer needs the time to create its magic. Trifle is eaten with the eyes first. On my 18th birthday, I was hanging out with the boys in the quadrangle at school when my eyes turned towards the school balcony and I saw my wife Johanne (Jojo) for the first time – it felt like a sudden electric slap. While courting, her big, brightly coloured trifles filled with adolescent layers of wobbly virescence, wine-coloured reds and buttery yellows made their way into my heart. To stand before a trifle at eye level is to remember the moment I first met Johanne. Now, at the ripe age of 71, I still love trifle: each mouthful takes me back to that moment.

At a long table under the Cumbrae pergola we sat with the full history of Sicily around us. I wasn't born in Sicily, but the food of my childhood has influenced how I cook today: it is at the heart of my cooking. At Cumbrae Farm our neighbours were also new Australians, with Dutch, German, New Zealand and Northern Italian heritage. The Van der Vliets and De Groots helped us plant our orchard with Gravenstein apples, which were the first crop we picked in late January to the middle of February. Mum learnt how to make traybake apple cake from Yvonne Smith, our Kiwi friend up the road. The Deckerskittas always offered a cup of coffee and milk with homemade pfeffernüsse and other spiced cookies that at the time were foreign to us. The Spizzos, across the road, came from the Treppo Grande comune in Friuli-Venezia Giulia region in northeast Italy. They spoke 'proper' Italian, we spoke a Sicilian village dialect. I never understood a word they said. To this day, two of their sons, Otto and Fabio, still call me Tommy (the name they called me until the age of 11). Mrs Spizzo's risotto was elegant, unfussy with no fancy garnishes, a gorgeous creamy bowl of goodness, a thousand treasures in one bowl.

The image of that table laden with numerous dialects still influences me with great chunks of affection – it's a concoction of alluring aromas and spirited saints.

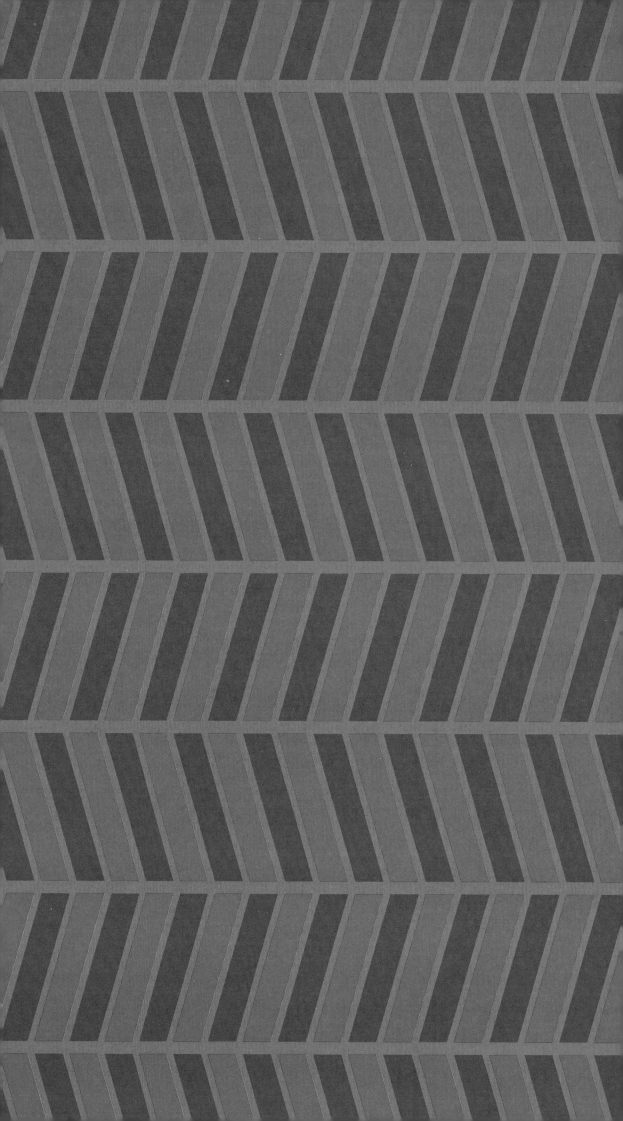

TACTUAL INTENT

Dear Raphael, Theodore, Otto and Leni, autumn is my favourite season. A rosella perched outside my bedroom window – a modern-day influencer decades before it became de rigueur – is perfectly comfortable zooming in fluoro green, blue, red and yellow. Cafe Leopard Boy is my alter ego, he is always changing colours, reinventing himself. He loves the sensuous fullness of everything: fashion shows, art galleries and gorgeous bookshops welcoming stars and misfits where boys meet boys and girls meet girls. It's like the kitchen at Cumbrae – a dream of autumn wildflowers scattered over my bed, a gentle, ordered chaos. Time is too languid to move.

A 'gothic' yellow-crested cockatoo with a decidedly punk attitude darts straight through the house and into the baroque Palazzo Borromeo on Isola Bella. Dividing its time between there and the couture fashion shows of Milan and Paris, firing up the crowd, finding fame on the cover of *Vogue* (April 2018). Its impressive lemon yellow pompadour like Marie Antoinette's, who wore hers under an elaborate headdress, is bold, rebellious, gravity-defying and oozes attitude and inspiration.

Farm rhythms continue to have effects decades after a career as a book designer and cafe owner. The traditional Sicilian food I ate at Cumbrae kept creeping into our cafe menu: bucatini Trapanese, eggs purgatory, arancini, *sfinciuni* (a Sicilian take on pizza from the Palermo region), fried bikini sandwiches wrapped in pancetta, pasta *alla norma* (with eggplant/aubergine), caponata bruschetta, *sarde beccafico* (stuffed sardines), squid ink spaghetti with prawns (shrimp), ricotta-filled cannoli and *sfinci* (Sicilian donuts) alongside banana bread, smashed avo and ricotta hotcakes.

A cafe is the town square, *la piazza*, a celebration of good food, tea, coffee, history, belonging and the best place for drawing, watching and *pranzo*.

Beds of chicory (endive), fennel and radish took pride of place in the garden, receiving all the attention. In summer and autumn, yellow-fleshed mariposa plums, along with apricots, quince, persimmon and fig trees struggled to be noticed beside the prickly pear. They needn't have bothered. The visual grandeur of prickly pear fruit – in jewel-like pinks with Greek green edges, Roman Empire yellow-orange and Monarch Vermilion – enjoyed a formidable reputation in those early Sicilian-Australian backyards of the 1950s.

The shape of prickly pear matched the glitter of the teardrop baubles hanging from the chandelier. With secateurs in hand and no gloves, Nonno Gaetano and Nonna Giuseppa cut and peeled each fruit with such ease, eating some as they went, then piling them into deep dishes, ready for us to eat.

prickly pear salad | Peel and slice 4 prickly pear fruits and put them into a bowl with 200 g (7 oz) halved black cherry tomatoes. Add the thin slices of 1 lemon, a few flat-leaf (Italian) parsley tops gone to seed, 3–5 torn mint leaves, a large pinch of caster sugar and drizzle with a little extra-virgin olive oil. Divide between four bowls, top with more chopped parsley or parsley gone to seed. Enough for 4.

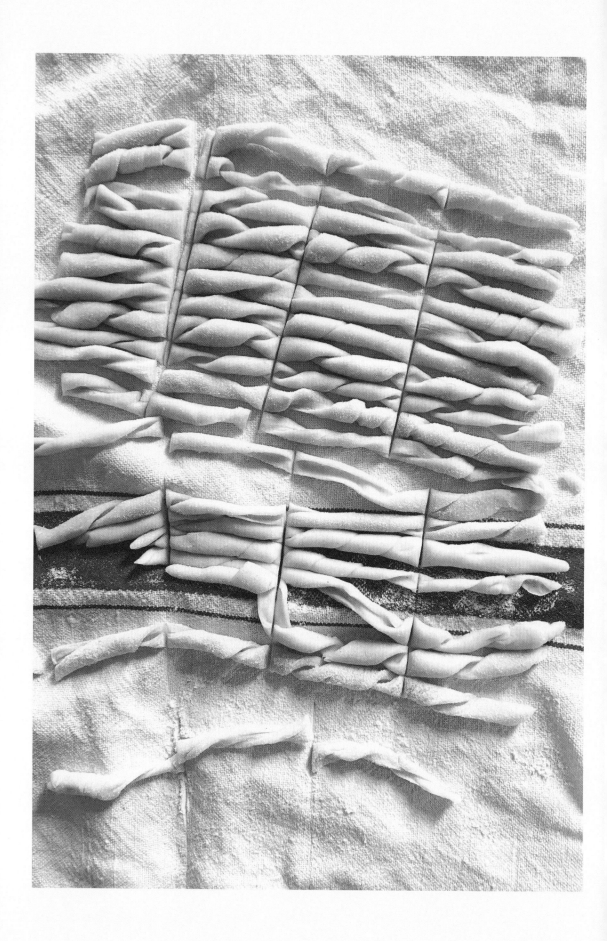

mushroom ragu casarecce

20 g (¾ oz) dried shiitake mushrooms, stems removed

20 g (¾ oz) dried porcini mushrooms

750 ml (25½ fl oz/3 cups) boiling water

80 ml (2½ fl oz/⅓ cup) extra-virgin olive oil

75 g (2¾ oz) salted butter, plus 25 g (1 oz) extra for the ragu

3 shallots, finely chopped

1 carrot, finely chopped

1 celery stalk, finely chopped

4 garlic cloves, finely chopped

200 g (7 oz) button mushrooms, some finely chopped, some quartered

200 g (7 oz) king brown (oyster) mushrooms, finely chopped

200 g (7 oz) fresh shiitake mushrooms, finely chopped

handful of thyme sprigs, leaves picked, plus extra to serve

1 bay leaf

1 batch fresh maccarruni pasta (see page 48), cut into 4–5 cm (1½–2 in) lengths to make casarecce

45 g (1½ oz) pecorino, freshly grated, plus extra to serve

salt and freshly ground black pepper

200 g (7 oz) soft goat's cheese, crumbled, to serve

enough for 4–6

Place the dried mushrooms in a heatproof bowl with the boiling water and cover with cling wrap. Soak for 30 minutes, then strain the liquid into another bowl to use in the ragu. Finely chop the mushrooms and set aside.

Heat the oil and butter in a large heavy-based saucepan over a medium heat, then fry the shallot, carrot, celery, garlic and season with salt and pepper and until the shallots are soft, about 8–10 minutes. Add all the fresh and dried mushrooms, the reserved mushroom stock, thyme and bay leaf and bring to the boil. Reduce to a low–medium heat and simmer for another 15 minutes. The sauce will start to thicken slightly. Add the extra butter at the end and stir through.

Meanwhile, bring a large saucepan of water to the boil, add salt and cook the casarecce. They will start to float to the top like gnocchi – let them float for about 1 minute, then scoop them out with a slotted spoon, reserving 125 ml (4 fl oz/½ cup) of the pasta water. Put the cooked casarecce back into the empty pan with the reserved pasta water, add the pecorino and stir well. Add the mushroom ragu and season with pepper.

Serve in warm bowls with the extra pecorino, crumbled goat's cheese and extra thyme leaves.

———

Cut the maccarruni into 4–5 cm (1½–2 in) lengths to match casarecce-style pasta. Set aside, ready to be cooked with the mushroom ragu. Alternatively, choose any one of the pesto-style sauces on page 33 to serve with the casarecce.

pappardelle
with almonds

6 garlic cloves, chopped

½ teaspoon salt

155 g (5½ oz/1 cup) roasted almonds, chopped,
  plus extra to serve

2 good handfuls of flat-leaf (Italian) parsley, chopped

90 g (3 oz) pecorino, freshly grated,
  plus extra to serve

100 ml (3½ fl oz/⅓ cup) extra-virgin olive oil

Semolina and water dough (page 34),
  cut into four portions

semolina flour, for dusting

juice of 1 lemon

freshly ground black pepper

enough for 4–6

Combine the garlic, salt, almonds and parsley in a food processor and pulse until a course texture is reached. Stir in the pecorino, then the oil. Set aside.

To make the pappardelle, take one portion of the dough and roll it out onto a floured bench. Use your hands to gently flatten the dough into an oval disk. Using a rolling pin, roll the dough out as thin as you can. Dust with semolina flour. Using a pizza wheel cutter, cut the dough into 1.5–2 cm (½–¾ in) wide ribbons and dust with semolina flour again. Repeat with the remaining dough.

Bring a large saucepan of water to the boil, add salt and cook the pappardelle. They will start to float to the top like gnocchi – let them float for about 1 minute, then drain, reserving 125 ml (4 fl oz/½ cup) of the pasta water. Put the cooked pappardelle back into the pan with the reserved pasta water. Stir the almond mixture, lemon juice and plenty of pepper through the pappardelle, then allow it to rest for a few minutes.

Serve in warm bowls with the extra chopped almonds and pecorino on top.

——

Before moving to Cumbrae Farm, all of Dad's family lived at the abandoned Tyneside Dairy in Box Hill, which had been known for its 'guaranteed' tubercular-free milk. The former dairy's milk room was where family weddings were celebrated. On these occasions branches of gum leaves were pinned to the walls, coloured streamers criss-crossed the ceiling and huge vases of flowers engulfed the tables. Bomboniere (white sugar-coated almonds) wrapped in diaphanous white lace bags that barely concealed their contents stood upright on large serving trays ready for the bride and groom to hand to each guest. In the make-shift kitchen beside the milk room, pappardelle – made that morning – lay drying on large wooden trays ready to be served after the antipasti. The room would burst to life during the bride and groom's first dance. On the playlist: Sicilian folk songs, Dean Martin, Frank Sinatra, Mario Lanza and Domenico Modugno singing 'Volare'.

At the farm, our Jersey cow, Mary, provided us with milk for our breakfast with enough left over to make cheese and ricotta. Flocks of Rhode Island reds and leghorns laid eggs for our favourite pastas and frittatas. On the kitchen table there was always a large, brightly patterned Sicilian dish filled with almonds in their shells. The decorative metal handles of the nutcracker fascinated me – it took every broken breath of strength to crack the shell to reveal the pearl inside.

mezzi rigatoni with broad beans, ricotta and zucchini

2 tablespoons extra-virgin olive oil

1 zucchini (courgette), thinly sliced into discs

400 g (14 oz) mezzi rigatoni

2–3 basil sprigs

Pangrattato (page 26)

250 g (9 oz/1 cup) smooth ricotta, to serve

broad beans

500 g (1 lb 2 oz/2¾ cups) dried broad (fava) beans, peeled

80 ml (2½ fl oz/⅓ cup) extra-virgin olive oil

1 large banana shallot or 2 shallots, finely chopped

5 tender wild fennel fronds or 1 bunch of dill stems

6 garlic cloves, peeled

2 litres (68 fl oz/8 cups) vegetable, chicken stock or water

1 Parmigiano Reggiano rind

salt and freshly ground black pepper

enough for 4–6

Soak the broad beans in 2 litres (68 fl oz/8 cups) of water overnight.

The next day, heat the oil in a large heavy-based saucepan over a medium heat. Add the shallots, fennel or dill, garlic, salt and pepper and fry until the shallots are soft, about 6–8 minutes. Add the drained broad beans and cook over a low heat for 15 minutes, stirring occasionally. Add the stock or water, raise the heat to medium and slowly bring to a simmer. Add the rind and partially cover the pan with a lid. Reduce the heat to low and cook for 45 minutes–1 hour. From time to time, use a potato masher to squash the broad beans so that by the end of cooking the sauce will be a chunky puree.

Meanwhile, heat the oil in a frying pan over a medium heat. Fry the zucchini until golden brown, about 8–10 minutes on each side. Season with salt and pepper and set aside.

Bring a large saucepan of water to the boil, add salt and cook the pasta until al dente.

Meanwhile, prepare the *pangrattato* by tearing the basil and mixing it through the breadcrumbs.

Drain the pasta when it is ready, reserving 125 ml (4 fl oz/½ cup) of the pasta water. Return the pasta to the saucepan with the reserved pasta water and add the broad bean sauce, stirring well. Rest the pasta for 5 minutes with the lid on.

Serve the pasta topped with spoonfuls of ricotta, fried zucchini and basil *pangrattato*.

———

In the garden, the last of the zucchini were combined with dried broad beans from the previous year and scattered with fresh basil, which was still producing plush silk green leaves.

linguine roast chicken

1 × 1.5 kg (3 lb 5 oz) free-range chicken

125 ml (4 fl oz/½ cup) mild olive oil

250 ml (8½ fl oz/1 cup) dry white wine

500 g (1 lb 2 oz) linguine

80 g (2¾ oz/½ cup) pine nuts, toasted,
   plus extra to serve

60 g (2 oz/½ cup) currants or raisins

2 long green chillies, cut into thin discs,
   plus extra to serve

100 g (3½ oz) baby cherry tomatoes,
   plus extra to serve

30 g (1 oz/1 cup) basil leaves, whole or torn

1 lemon, cut into quarters, to serve

125 g (4½ oz/½ cup) Basil and spinach pesto
   (page 33), to serve

stuffing

150 g (5½ oz) salted butter, softened

juice of 2 lemons, squeezed lemon halves reserved

3 garlic cloves, crushed

salt and freshly ground black pepper

enough for 4–6

Preheat the oven to 180°C (360°F) and place a wire rack into a roasting tin.

For the stuffing, combine the butter, lemon juice, garlic, salt and pepper in a small bowl and set aside.

Wash the chicken inside and out and pat dry with paper towel. Trim away any excess fat. Starting near the chicken's neck, gently insert your fingers under the skin and push your fingers through to separate it from the breast and thigh meat. The skin should remain attached but loosened. Rub the stuffing beneath the skin, inside the cavities and all over the outside. Place the chicken, breast side up, on the wire rack. Put the reserved squeezed lemon halves into the cavity and pour the oil into the cavity and over the chicken. Pour the wine over the top and roast for 50–60 minutes, until the skin is golden brown. Remove the chicken and cool a little while keeping the pan juices warm.

Bring a large saucepan of water to the boil, add salt and cook the pasta until al dente.

While the pasta is cooking, work quickly to shred the chicken and return the meat to the roasting tin.

Drain the pasta and toss it into the roasting tin with the chicken. Add the pine nuts, currants, chillies, tomatoes and basil and mix well, scraping any residue from the side and bottom of the pan.

Divide the pasta into individual bowls and top with the extra pine nuts, some extra tomatoes, chillies, lemon wedges and pesto.

—

Nigella Lawson, earthquakes, volcanoes, autumn, fire and swimming have all inspired this dish as have, of course, my love for Sicily and the perfect Sunday lunch. This roast chook comes together wrapped up like a Hervé Koubi ballet.

chicken chops
with chickpeas

80 ml (2½ fl oz/⅓ cup) extra-virgin olive oil,
plus extra to drizzle

12 chicken thigh fillets, skin on,
patted dry with paper towel

3 tablespoons dry white wine

2 × 425 g (15 oz) tinned chickpeas,
drained and rinsed

8 garlic cloves, whole, peeled

2 teaspoons ground turmeric

2 teaspoons smoked paprika

¼ teaspoon chilli flakes

1 red capsicum (bell pepper), core, membrane
and seeds removed and cut into strips

small handful of flat-leaf (Italian)
parsley sprigs, chopped

grated zest and juice of 1 lemon

30 g (1 oz) salted butter, chopped into 12 pieces

salt and freshly ground black pepper

herby yoghurt

500 g (1 lb 2 oz/2 cups) Greek-style yoghurt

1 garlic clove, crushed

handful of each of mint, basil, parsley,
thyme leaves and chives, torn

grated zest of 1 lemon

salt

enough for 6–8

Preheat the oven to 200°C (390°F). Use 2 tablespoons of the oil to grease a 28 × 38 cm (11 × 15 in) roasting tin.

Heat the remaining oil in a large frying pan over a medium–high heat. Season the chicken with salt and pepper and cook in batches for 8–10 minutes on each side, just until it starts to get some colour. Set the chicken aside in a bowl. Pour the wine into the hot pan and boil for about 1 minute, stirring to scrape off any bits. Take off the heat and pour the wine over the chicken.

Combine the chickpeas, garlic, turmeric, paprika, chilli flakes, capsicum, parsley and lemon zest and juice in a large bowl and mix well. Put the chickpea mixture into the roasting tin and spread over the bottom. Push the chicken into the chickpea mixture, pouring any juices over the top. Place a chunk of butter on top of each piece of chicken and season with salt and pepper. Roast for about 45 minutes. Remove the roasting tin from the oven and tilt it to one corner to collect some of the juices, then spoon the juices over the chicken. Cover with foil and rest for 20 minutes.

For the herby yoghurt, mix the yoghurt with the garlic and spread it over a flat dish. Sprinkle with the herbs, lemon zest and salt and drizzle a little extra oil on top.

Present the chicken on a large dish for everyone to help themselves. Serve with herby yoghurt.

—

There is nothing sweeter nor more life-affirming than the smell of spiced, roasting chicken. The chickpeas in this dish are like hundreds of golden beads edging in and around the chicken. When I was a child, Nonna Giuseppa and Mum called me *Sango mio* (my blood). Nonna and Mum may not have considered this dish traditional – the many ingredients may have amused them – but like Rembrandt's portrait of Margaretha de Geer, I see them both facing me directly, telling me to be active, engaged and loving my chicken with chickpeas for *pranzo*.

The annual Eastern Peninsula School sports day was held at the Hastings football ground. This event was taken very seriously by Sister Francis. Her resilience and hardworking lessons as sports coach were bordering on full-scale *manicomio*. Sister Francis was not afraid to roll up her sleeves and brown tunic to demonstrate the long jump. Her run-up, leap and bounce danced across the sky like an emerging murmuration of a swirling aerial ballet – flapping brown tunic, white coif, rosary beads and with guimpe cloth twisting and twirling around her neck and shoulders.

The 'Eastern' was held in the middle of March, not long after the summer break. Training times were crucial in the lead up to the event. Being the tallest, oldest boy, I was in a few team sports – tunnel ball, corner spry, the 50 m potato sack relay race and the 400 m relay dash. The final event of the day was the marching parade where each school was judged on their skill, uniformity and timing, especially on the turns. I will never forget 1963 – this was the year I won the blue ribbon for the fastest boy in the individual potato sack race. I put this down to extra training after school on the farm. The trick is to have the lightest potato sack and not to hold it too tight. Toes should be tucked right into the corners, hop fast and have Sister Francis at the finishing line screaming, holding and shimmying her head from side to side.

pork belly with quince | In a large bowl, combine 1 × 1 kg (2 lb 3 oz) pork belly, cut into four portions, 250 ml (8½ fl oz/1 cup) chicken stock, 250 ml (8½ fl oz/1 cup) port, 500 ml (17 fl oz/2 cups) red wine, 1 tablespoon balsamic vinegar, 3 garlic bulbs, halved vertically, 4 thyme sprigs, 3 bay leaves, 1 tablespoon fennel seeds, 4 quinces, halved horizontally (skin on), 4 whole shallots (skin on) and 1 chopped brown onion and season with salt and freshly ground black pepper. Cover and marinate for at least 5 hours or overnight, turning the meat from time to time. Preheat the oven to 180°C (360°F). Remove the pork from the marinade and pat it dry with paper towel. Reserve the marinade. Dust the pork with plain flour. Heat 3 tablespoons of mild olive oil in a large, shallow, enamelled cast-iron casserole pot with a lid over a medium–high heat. Brown the pork pieces on both sides, about 8–10 minutes. Pour the marinade into the pot and roast with the lid on for 3 hours. Rest for 15–20 minutes, cover and keep warm. Meanwhile, blanch 200 g (7 oz) green beans for 3 minutes. Serve the pork belly with the blanched green beans, drizzled with extra-virgin olive oil and seasoned with salt and freshly ground black pepper. Enough for 4.

tomato tart

Simple cos salad (page 123), to serve

sour cream pastry

200 g (7 oz) chilled salted butter

250 g (9 oz/1⅔ cups) plain (all-purpose) flour, plus extra for dusting

80 ml (2½ fl oz/⅓ cup) sour cream

filling

3 tablespoons mild olive oil

3 tablespoons white-wine vinegar

3 shallots, chopped

2 eggs

150 ml (5 fl oz) pouring (single/light) cream

1 spring onion (scallion), finely chopped

45 g (1½ oz) pecorino, freshly grated

200 g (7 oz/1 cup) smooth ricotta

200 g (7 oz/1 cup) mascarpone

100 g (3½ oz) baby English spinach leaves, finely sliced

30 g (1 oz/1 cup) basil leaves

1 tablespoon baby capers

500 g (1 lb 2 oz) cherry tomatoes, some halved but most left whole

125 g (4½ oz/1 cup) pitted black olives

salt and freshly ground black pepper

enough for 6–8

To make the pastry, pulse the butter and flour in a food processor until the mixture resembles breadcrumbs. Add the sour cream and pulse until the dough just comes together to just form a ball. Press down on the dough to form a flat disc, then wrap it in cling wrap. Refrigerate for 1 hour. Remove the pastry at least 20 minutes before using.

Grease the base and side of a 26 cm (10¼ in) fluted loose-based flan (tart) tin with butter and dust with flour. On a floured work surface, roll the pastry out to around 40 cm (15¾ in) in diameter and roughly 6 mm (¼ in) thick. Line the prepared tin with the pastry, leaving it overhanging the edge. Cover with cling wrap and refrigerate for 1 hour. (If you are making the tart in advance you can freeze it at this stage.)

Preheat the oven to 180°C (360°F).

Cover the pastry with aluminium foil and fill it with baking beads or dried beans. Bake for 20 minutes, remove the foil and beads, then bake for a further 5 minutes. Let the pie cool for 20 minutes, then trim the edge.

For the filling, heat the oil in a frying pan over a low heat, then add the vinegar and shallots. Fry until the shallots are translucent, about 8–10 minutes. Set aside to cool.

Combine the eggs, cream, spring onion, pecorino, ricotta, mascarpone, spinach, basil and capers and salt and pepper in a large bowl and mix well.

Spread the shallots over the base, then add the cream mixture and top with the olives and half of the tomatoes. Bake for 40–45 minutes, or until the top is set and golden brown. Top with the remaining tomatoes. Allow the tart to cool a little before removing from the tin.

Let the tart cool for a further 10–15 minutes before serving with the Simple cos salad. This tart is also great to take on a picnic.

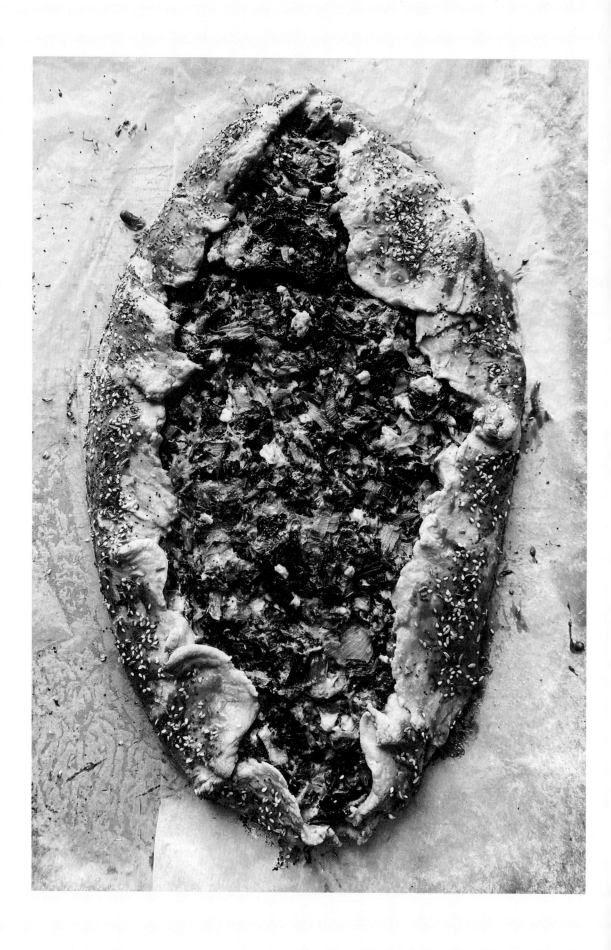

silverbeet and taleggio crostata

Sour cream pastry (page 120)

1 egg lightly beaten together with 1 tablespoon of milk, for brushing the pastry

3 tablespoons mixed seeds, such as sesame, poppy and fennel

filling

2 tablespoons extra-virgin olive oil

30 g (1 oz) salted butter

1 brown onion, diced

1 leek, halved lengthways, rinsed and sliced into 5 mm (¼ in) discs

1 bunch silverbeet (Swiss chard), stalks removed

400 g (14 oz) baby English spinach leaves

4 eggs, whisked

375 g (13 oz/1½ cups) smooth ricotta

200 g (7 oz) taleggio, torn into small pieces

45 g (1½ oz) pecorino, freshly grated

30 g (1 oz/1 cup) flat-leaf (Italian) parsley, chopped

salt and freshly ground black pepper

simple cos salad

2 small cos (romaine) lettuces, trimmed and halved lengthways

juice of ½ lemon

extra-virgin olive oil, to drizzle

white-wine vinegar, to drizzle

1 tablespoon baby capers

pecorino, freshly grated, to serve

enough for 4

Follow the recipe on page 120 to make the pastry, but pulse the dough until it just forms a ball. Wrap the dough in cling wrap and refrigerate for 30 minutes.

For the filling, heat the oil and butter in a large frying pan over a low heat, then gently fry the onion and leek until soft, about 8–10 minutes. Set aside to cool. Boil the silverbeet leaves for 3 minutes in a large saucepan of salted water. Remove the leaves and squeeze out any water. Blanch the spinach in the same water for around 1 minute, then squeeze out any water and set aside.

Combine the cooked onion, leek, silverbeet, spinach, egg, ricotta, taleggio, pecorino, parsley, salt and pepper in a large bowl and mix well.

Preheat the oven to 180°C (360°F). Grease a large baking tray and line it with baking paper.

To assemble the tart, on a lightly floured surface, roll the pastry into an oval shape, roughly measuring 33 × 52 cm (13 × 20½ in) and 5 mm (¼ in) thick. Place the pastry on the prepared baking tray. Spread the filling over the base of the pastry, leaving a 7–10 cm (2¾–4 in) edge around it. Gently fold the outer edge of the pastry up and over the top of the filling and press softly with both hands. Brush the pastry with the beaten egg and milk and sprinkle the seeds on top. Bake for 45 minutes–1 hour, or until the top is set and golden brown.

Serve the tart warm with a salad of cos lettuce drizzled with the lemon juice, oil and vinegar and sprinkled with the baby capers and a light dusting of pecorino.

———

Keep the silverbeet stalks for a spring minestrone. Mum always said it was the stalks that were the secret to her minestrone, adding flavour without complicating the other vegetables.

124

apple and
red grape pie

1 egg lightly beaten together with 1 tablespoon
  of milk, for brushing the pastry

pastry

300 g (10½ oz/2 cups) self-raising flour

300 g (10½ oz/2 cups) plain (all-purpose) flour

250 g (9 oz) salted butter, cut into small cubes

185 ml (6 fl oz/¾ cup) boiling water

filling

1.5 kg (3 lb 5 oz) peeled and quartered
  granny smith apples (or any other tart
  cooking apple)

115 g (4 oz/½ cup) caster sugar

50 g (1¾ oz/½ cup) soft brown sugar

½ teaspoon ground cinnamon

6 cloves

1 star anise

good pinch of freshly grated nutmeg

grated zest and juice of 1 lemon

150 g (5½ oz) red grapes

125 ml (4 fl oz/½ cup) dry vermouth

enough for 8

For the pastry, combine the flours in a food processor and pulse to mix well. Add the butter and pulse until the mixture resembles coarse breadcrumbs. Pour in the water and pulse until just combined. Turn the pastry out onto a lightly floured bench and cut it into two pieces, one slightly bigger than the other. Press the pastry into discs and wrap them in cling wrap. Rest for at least 30 minutes.

For the filling, combine the apples, sugars, cinnamon, cloves, star anise, nutmeg, lemon zest and juice in a heavy-based saucepan and cook, uncovered, over a medium heat for 20 minutes. Add the grapes and vermouth and cook for another 5 minutes. Take off the heat and cool, discarding the cloves and star anise. Set aside to cool.

Preheat the oven to 180°C (360°F). Grease a 26 cm (10¼ in) round pie dish, 5 cm (2 in) deep, with butter.

Roll out the larger piece of pastry to 35 cm (13¾ in) round and about 5 mm (¼ in) thick. Don't be alarmed if the pastry breaks off in parts – this is a rustic-style pastry and it's all part of the charm. Place the pastry into the prepared pie dish, overlapping or pinching pieces together as needed. Fill the pastry with the cooled filling and top with the remaining pastry. Again, position the pastry as best you can, then pinch the edges to join. Brush the top with the egg and milk mixture. Cut four lines in the top then bake for 45–50 minutes, or until golden brown. Set aside for 15 minutes to cool before serving.

———

Jojo's secret pastry recipe is a gorgeous, simple, hot water pastry for sweet or savoury pies and tarts. You can play around with different shapes to top your creation, such as hearts or stars.

AUTUMN

rhubarb, fig and almond cake

6 rhubarb stalks, trimmed and chopped into bite-sized pieces

8 fresh plump figs, halved, plus extra to serve (optional)

50 g (1¾ oz/½ cup) flaked almonds

mascarpone or thick (double/heavy) cream, to serve

compote

200 g (7 oz/¾ cup) caster sugar

4–5 young fig leaves

cake batter

250 ml (8½ fl oz/1 cup) mild olive oil

2 eggs

pinch of salt

grated zest of 1 orange

1 tablespoon dry marsala

150 g (5½ oz/⅔ cup) caster sugar

300 g (10½ oz/2 cups) self-raising flour, sifted

enough for 8

Preheat the oven to 180°C (360°F). Grease a 24 cm (9½ in) round cake tin with butter and line with baking paper. Place a third of the rhubarb pieces into the base of the prepared cake tin.

To make the compote, combine the sugar and 200 ml (7 fl oz) of water in a small saucepan and bring to the boil over medium heat. Turn the heat down to low and stir until the sugar dissolves. Add the fig leaves and the remaining rhubarb pieces and simmer until the rhubarb is tender, about 3–4 minutes. Remove from the heat and cool.

To make the cake batter, whisk the oil, eggs, salt, orange zest, marsala and sugar in a large bowl with a balloon whisk until well combined. Add the flour and mix with a wooden spoon until just combined.

Arrange the halved figs around the perimeter of the cake tin with the cut side pressed to the baking paper. Pour the cake batter into the tin on top of the rhubarb. Sprinkle the almonds over the top and bake for about 50 minutes, or until it tests done with a skewer. Leave the cake to cool completely in the tin.

Place the cake on a serving plate and serve with the extra figs, compote and mascarpone or cream.

This cake will keep for up to 3 days stored in an airtight container.

———

Like my dad, Johanne's father, Vincenzo, had a variety of fig trees growing in his garden. After a month of Johanne and I going out without our parents' knowledge, I decided to turn up at her front door only to be greeted by Vincenzo. Needless to say, there was no way I would be seeing his youngest daughter again until he met my parents. One week later, both Sicilian families met. Their food was different and yet familiar at the same time. After four years of courting, we had a traditional Sicilian wedding. Six weeks later Jo was pregnant. Ten weeks later, and just before Easter, we ran away to Canberra where I was offered a job. It was the perfect honeymoon. Besides our clothes and one armchair, we took fresh figs from Vincenzo and Diego's gardens with us on the long road trip to our nation's capital.

hazelnut cake

Ganache (page 211) or Nutella, to serve (optional)

thick (double/heavy) cream, to serve

cake batter

200 g (7 oz/1⅓ cups) self-raising flour

150 g (5½ oz/⅔ cup) soft brown sugar

150 g (5½ oz/1⅓ cups) ground hazelnuts

grated zest and juice 1 orange

4 eggs

250 ml (8½ fl oz/1 cup) grapeseed oil

250 g (9 oz/1 cup) Greek-style yoghurt

2 teaspoons natural vanilla extract

3 tablespoons gin

hazelnut praline

120 g (4½ oz) toasted hazelnuts, roughly chopped

180 g (6½ oz/¾ cup) caster sugar

hazelnut crystals

120 g (4½ oz/1 cup) toasted hazelnuts, roughly chopped

180 g (6½ oz/¾ cup) caster sugar

enough for 8–10

Preheat the oven to 165°C (325°F). Grease a 23 cm (9 in) round cake tin with butter and line with baking paper.

To make the cake batter, combine the flour, brown sugar, ground hazelnuts and orange zest in a large bowl and mix well. In another bowl, combine the eggs, oil, yoghurt, vanilla extract, gin and orange juice and mix well. Now add the wet mixture to the dry and stir in well. Pour the batter into the prepared tin and bake for 50 minutes, or until it tests done with a skewer. Allow to cool in the tin for 30 minutes before turning out onto a wire rack to cool completely.

Meanwhile, to make the hazelnut praline, spread the nuts over a baking tray lined with baking paper. Stir the caster sugar and 80 ml (2½ fl oz/⅓ cup) of water in a small saucepan over medium heat until the sugar dissolves. Increase the heat to high and, without stirring, allow the mixture to boil until it turns an amber colour, about 6–8 minutes. Remove from the heat and carefully pour the hot syrup over the nuts. Allow the praline to cool completely before breaking into shards.

To make the crystals, increase the oven to 180°C (360°F) and line a baking tray with baking paper. Combine the hazelnuts, caster sugar and 80 ml (2½ fl oz/⅓ cup) of water in a small bowl, then spread the mixture out over the prepared baking tray. Bake in the oven for about 35–40 minutes, or until crystals start to form. Allow it to cool completely before breaking into crystals.

If using, spread the ganache over the top of the cake. Top the cake with large chunks of praline and scatter over the crystals. Serve with dollops of cream.

This cake will keep for up to 2 days stored in an airtight container (if you're making this cake ahead of time, apply the ganache and praline on the day you are serving.).

—

The chefs in my cafe always made praline to decorate our cakes. In my first attempt at making it, I inadvertently made what I call 'crystals'. They look amazing sprinkled over a cake.

mascarpone cheesecake | Preheat the oven to 160°C (320°F). Grease a 22 cm (8¾ in) springform pan with butter and line with baking paper. In a food processor, pulse 400 g (14 oz) broken gingernut (ginger snap) biscuits to a fine texture, then add 200 g (7 oz) melted salted butter and process until well combined. Gently press the mixture over the base and side of the prepared tin using your hands. Refrigerate while you prepare the filling. In the bowl of an electric mixer with the paddle attachment, beat 500 g (1 lb 2 oz/2¼ cups) each of mascarpone and cream cheese, both at room temperature, with 200 g (7 oz/¾ cup) caster sugar until well combined. Add 1 teaspoon natural vanilla extract, the grated zest and juice of 1 lime and beat until just combined. Now use the whisk attachment to incorporate 4 eggs, one at a time, mixing well after each addition. Pour the batter into the tin. Bake for 1 hour, or until the top is a light golden brown. Turn the oven off and let the cheesecake rest in the oven for about 30 minutes with the door ajar. Best served warm with warmed Roasted plums with vincotto and chilli (right). Alternatively, it will keep for up to 2 days stored in an airtight container in the refrigerator. It will be still beautiful. Enough for 8–10.

roasted plums with vincotto and chilli | Preheat the oven to 200°C (390°F) and line a baking tray with baking paper. Put 700 g (1 lb 9 oz) satsuma or blood plums and 350 g (12½ oz) sugar plums on the tray. Add 30 g (1 oz) thinly sliced fresh ginger, 1 long red chilli, halved lengthways, 5 cloves, 3 star anise and 1 cinnamon stick. Drizzle with 2 tablespoons date syrup and 2 tablespoons vincotto. Roast for about 25 minutes, until the skins just start to come away from the plums. (It all adds to the decadent look.) Serve warm or cold on toast, brioche, over warm bowls of porridge, on fluffy hotcakes or with your favourite tea cake or cheesecake. Enough for 4–6.

mel's hazelnut and orange biscotti

3 egg whites, at room temperature

250 g (9 oz/2¼ cups) ground hazelnuts

100 g (3½ oz/1 cup) almond flour

250 g (9 oz/1 cup) caster sugar

2 teaspoons natural hazelnut extract

grated zest of 1 orange

150 g (5½ oz/1 cup) icing (confectioners') sugar, for coating

160 g (5¾ oz/½ cup) good quality marmalade, or Ganache (page 211) or Nutella

makes 24

Preheat the oven to 180°C (360°F) and line a baking tray with baking paper.

Lightly whisk the egg whites with a fork in a large bowl until light and frothy, then add the ground hazelnuts, almond flour, caster sugar, hazelnut extract and orange zest and mix well.

Sift the icing sugar into a separate bowl, ready for coating the biscotti.

Roll a heaped tablespoon of biscotti dough into a ball, then coat the ball in icing sugar. Place the balls on the prepared baking tray and squash or press down on each ball with your thumb, creating a well in the centre of each biscotti and also a few cracks. Bake for 20–25 minutes, or until the biscotti are lightly brown on top and golden underneath. Transfer to a wire rack to cool.

Place a heaped ¼ teaspoon of marmalade onto each biscotti. Alternatively, fill with Ganache (page 211) or Nutella. Or do half with marmalade and the other half with ganache.

These biscotti will keep for up to a week stored in an airtight container.

—

I first met Melanie Russo when she attended kinder with my daughter Pam, so I have known her a long time. Melanie's big, bold cooking smacks you in the mouth. My father started working for the Russo brothers, Joe and Jack (distant cousins to Mel's family), in the early 1950s. Joe, Jack and Diego bought a farm in Tyabb called Cumbrae. I first met Mel's father, Tony, in year 7 at tech school. His parents, David and Cathy, supplied my cafe with an abundance of herbs and vegetables. Jack's daughter Teresa is married to Ange, who is my son Paul's godfather. Joe's son Tom did all the cabinetry work at the cafe. The names Russo and Mirabella have been entwined for generations in one form or another; their children have been playing together for years. Mel's biscotti recipe is a treasure to savour with every bite.

THE INTERIM WHAT

Dear Raphael, Theodore, Otto and Leni,
winter is my favourite season. At the pointy
end of Cumbrae Farm was our own little surf
beach, where carolling magpies lived, nipping
the fingers and toes of those who said 'Boo!'
through the marshes. The coastline was
filled with centuries of stories and nature
loomed in greys, hues of Neptune blues and
yellow-stained greens. Our winter beach was
wild brushstrokes of raucous colours like
fauvist paintings. Mountains of abandoned
seashells were reused in silhouettes for
runway-recycled jewellery, forcing us
underwater like mermen and returning to
shore from the water's power. We were reborn
into the '50s instrumental surf rock band
The Centurians, strumming our air guitars
to their song 'Intoxia'.

The autumn days may have gone but winter still had its fair
share of weekend visitors. The table at Cumbrae was always
set with small white-and-green enamel plates laden with olives,
while shiny wedding-gift crockery in assorted colours and
patterns were filled with hard cheeses, polpette and cold-cut
meats. On the mantelpiece above the open fire and next to the
stove, statues of the Holy Family rested on deep blood red shades
of burgundy cloth. Shadows from the Chiesa della Madonna di
Giubino merged with couples hemmed in foamy blue French
pigments; a girl on horseback is looking for the man; angels
blow trumpets unlocking a foreign language.

      Every cook has their own favourite family version
of *ragu alla bolognese*. Mum's recipe is perfect to use for lasagne
and other baked pasta dishes. I had grown up thinking *ragu
alla bolognese* was a Calatafimi dish cooked by my family and
our relations. It had never occurred to me, until attending art
school, that other people had their own family version as well,
even the Aussies. There is no such thing as the best bolognese –
because the best *ragu alla bolognese* is Mum's, the one we ate at
Cumbrae with ravioli, maccarruni or in lasagne. Mum's lasagne
always included shaved mortadella and peas between the layers.
Bechamel never graced Mum's kitchen, nor creamy sauces
of any kind.

Mum was always the last to be seated, grasping her chair, surveying the scene on and around the table. Mum and Dad's sign of the cross was the signal to tuck in. My memories of her are dominated by this kitchen ritual: Dad the first to be served at the head of the table, me sitting to his left, Mum opposite me. Frank, the second to be served, sat at the other head with Josie to his left and Rosa to his right, beside me. These days I prefer to sit in the middle of the table whenever my children and grandbabies – all twelve of us – gather. If anyone, it is Leni, my youngest grandbaby, in her highchair, who sits at the head of the table, commanding life around her.

pina's *ragu alla bolognese* (bolognese sauce) Fry 750 g (1 lb 11 oz) minced (ground) beef and 250 g (9 oz) minced (ground) pork in a large saucepan over a medium heat (with no oil), breaking up any lumps with a wooden spoon, until slightly browned. Remove from the pan and set aside. Discard any liquid left behind. Heat 80 ml (2½ fl oz/⅓ cup) mild olive oil in the same pan, then add 1 diced brown onion and cook over a low heat until translucent, around 8–10 minutes. Add 2 crushed garlic cloves and cook for 30 seconds–1 minute, until the mixture is golden. Add the meat, 1 teaspoon dried oregano and 125 ml (4 fl oz/½ cup) marsala and season with salt and freshly ground black pepper. Stir thoroughly and fry for 1 minute more. Add 3 × 700 g (1 lb 9 oz) jars of tomato passata (pureed tomatoes), 1 tablespoon white (granulated) sugar and 1½ passata jars of water (swirling to release the tomato residue from the jars), stir and bring to the boil. Reduce the heat to low–medium and simmer the sauce for about 45–60 minutes, uncovered, until it has thickened slightly, but is not too thick. Makes 3 litres (101 fl oz).

pina's lasagne

100 ml (3½ fl oz) mild olive oil

1 small brown onion, diced

250 g (9 oz/1⅔ cups) fresh or frozen peas,
plus extra to serve

handful of Japanese breadcrumbs

Pina's *ragu alla bolognese* (page 139), warmed

8–10 store-bought fresh lasagne sheets or
Flour and water dough (page 34) or
500 g (1 lb 2 oz) dried lasagne sheets

500 g (1 lb 2 oz) mozzarella, shredded

250 g (9 oz) freshly shaved green olive mortadella

3 eggs, lightly beaten

250 g (9 oz) Parmigiano Reggiano, freshly grated,
plus extra to serve

salt and freshly ground black pepper

enough for 8–10

Preheat the oven to 180°C (360°F).

Heat 2 tablespoons oil in a saucepan over a low heat, then gently fry the onion until translucent, about 5 minutes. Stir in the peas, season with salt and pepper, and mix well. Add 125 ml (4 fl oz/½ cup) of water and simmer with the lid on until the peas are tender, around 5 minutes.

Grease a baking dish with the remaining oil, sprinkle with the breadcrumbs, then cover the base with 500–750 ml (17–25½ fl oz/2–3 cups) of the bolognese sauce.

Bring a large saucepan of water to the boil, add salt, then blanch the lasagne sheets (regardless of which type you decide to use) for 3–4 minutes, or until soft enough to handle. Drain, then do what Mum does, and rest over the side of the pot or put them into a large bowl with a little olive oil stirred through the sheets to stop them from sticking together. You could also put straight into cold water, then drain and pat dry.

Place a layer of lasagne sheets on top of the sauce, then spread more sauce over the top of the sheets. Spread shredded mozzarella over the top, then some slices of mortadella, some of the peas, drizzle with the egg and sprinkle with the Parmigiano Reggiano. Repeat the layers, ending with the bolognese sauce, shredded mozzarella, a few peas and cheese. Lay a sheet of baking paper, then foil, on top of the lasagne and bake for 30 minutes. Remove the baking paper and foil and cook for another 15–20 minutes, until it is all golden and bubbly with crusty edges. Rest the lasagne for 15 minutes. Garnish with Parmigiano Reggiano and serve with peas, if you like. Below is a recipe for *besciamelle* (bechamel) if that's your thing.

———

besciamelle (**bechamel**) Gently heat 100 g (3½ oz) salted butter in a saucepan over a medium heat until melted, then begin to whisk in 100 g (3½ oz/⅔ cup) plain (all-purpose) flour. Cook until the mixture starts to bubble, about 30–60 seconds, and becomes a thick paste (roux). Gradually whisk 1 litre (34 fl oz/4 cups) of hot full-cream (whole) milk into the roux while slowly bringing it to the boil until it thickens to become a smooth, white sauce. Reduce the heat to low, add 75 g (2¾ oz) Parmigiano Reggiano, 2 thyme sprigs or 1 bay leaf (or both), a pinch of grated nutmeg, salt and freshly ground black pepper (to taste) and cook, stirring, for another 2 minutes. Set aside ready to use. Makes just over 1 litre (34 fl oz/4 cups).

cafe cannelloni bolognese

500 g (1 lb 2 oz) minced (ground) beef

250 g (9 oz) minced (ground) pork

3 tablespoons mild olive oil

60 g (2 oz) salted butter, plus extra to serve

1 brown onion, finely chopped

1 carrot, finely chopped

1 celery stalk, finely chopped

4 garlic cloves, crushed

pinch of chilli flakes

100 g (3½ oz) pancetta, finely chopped

250 ml (8½ fl oz/1 cup) dry marsala

90 g (3 oz/⅓ cup) tomato paste (concentrated puree)

2 × 400 g (14 oz) tinned chopped tomatoes

chunk of Parmigiano Reggiano rind

pinch of finely grated nutmeg

1 bay leaf

3–4 thyme sprigs, leaves picked

3–4 oregano sprigs, leaves picked or
  1 tablespoon dried oregano

400 g (14 oz) dried cannelloni

salt and freshly ground black pepper

freshly grated Parmigiano Reggiano, to serve

enough for 6–8

Brown the meat in a deep, heavy-based saucepan over a medium–high heat. Remove from the pan and set aside. Discard any liquid left behind.

Heat the oil and butter in the same pan over a medium heat. Add the onion, carrot, celery, garlic, chilli and pancetta, and stir frequently until the vegetables are soft, about 6–8 minutes. Add the marsala and stir vigorously for 10–12 minutes, until all the liquid has been absorbed. Add in the tomato paste and stir for 2 minutes, then add the tinned tomatoes with 1 tin of water (swirling to release any tomato residue). Return the meat to the pan, then add the rind, nutmeg, all the herbs and season with salt and pepper. Bring the sauce to the boil, then lower the heat to low–medium and allow it to simmer with the lid slightly ajar for 1½ hours, stirring occasionally.

Bring a large saucepan of water to the boil, add salt, then cook the cannelloni until al dente. Drain and return the cannelloni to the saucepan with the extra butter and mix some bolognese through. Add the remaining bolognese and gently stir. Cover the pan and allow it to rest for a few minutes.

Serve in warm bowls topped with grated Parmigiano Reggiano.

———

In the cafe world I was surrounded by many talented chefs and cooks who brought their own ragu bolognese to the table. The recipe above is one I have made many times. One day I will go to Bologna and order *ragu alla bolognese* and I know I will love it. Pasta is comfort food like no other. The thought of a big bowl of pasta bolognese in all its richness quickens my pulse, feeds my soul and keeps me happy for a long time.

spaghettini with chicken bolognese

3 tablespoons mild olive oil

30 g (1 oz) salted butter, plus extra for the mushrooms

1 brown onion, finely chopped

1 carrot, finely chopped

1 celery stalk, finely chopped

4 garlic cloves, sliced

pinch of chilli flakes, plus extra to serve

2–3 sprigs each of thyme and rosemary, plus a little extra thyme, to serve

1 bay leaf

pinch of finely grated nutmeg

50 g (1¾ oz) pancetta, chopped (optional)

750 g (1 lb 11 oz) minced (ground) chicken or 2 skinless chicken breasts and 2 skinless thigh fillets, chopped then ground in a food processor to a course texture

200 g (7 oz) portobello mushrooms, diced

2 tablespoons sweet soy sauce

250 ml (8½ fl oz/1 cup) dry marsala

2 tablespoons tomato paste (concentrated puree)

3 large tomatoes, grated, or 2 × 400 g (14 oz) tinned chopped tomatoes

150 g (5½ oz) shimeji mushrooms, rinsed and trimmed

500 g (1 lb 2 oz) dry spaghettini

salt and freshly ground black pepper

250 g (9 oz/1 cup) mascarpone, to serve

175 g (6 oz/1 cup) Sicilian olives, to serve

freshly grated Parmigiano Reggiano, to serve

enough for 4–6

Heat the oil and butter in a large heavy-based saucepan over medium heat, then add the onion, carrot, celery, garlic, chilli flakes, herbs, bay leaf, nutmeg, salt, pepper and fry until the vegetables are soft, about 6–8 minutes. Add the pancetta, chicken and portobello mushrooms and stir, breaking up any clumps with a wooden spoon. Fry until the chicken is white, around 6–8 minutes. Stir in the soy sauce, then the marsala, cooking vigorously until the liquid has reduced by half and the alcohol smell has gone, about 6–8 minutes. Add the tomato paste and stir for 2 minutes, then add the tomatoes. Bring to the boil, then simmer for 40 minutes, stirring occasionally. Add the shimeji mushrooms and cook for a further 5 minutes. Remove from the heat and cover to keep warm.

Meanwhile, bring a large saucepan of water to the boil, add salt and cook the spaghettini until al dente. Reserve 125 ml (4 fl oz/½ cup) of the pasta water, then drain the pasta. Add the spaghettini to the bolognese and stir to combine. Cover the pan and allow it to rest for a few minutes.

While the pasta is resting, mix 1–2 tablespoons of the reserved pasta water with the mascarpone in a small bowl until it is light and creamy. You may need to add a little more water, depending on the thickness of the mascarpone – some brands can be thicker than others.

Divide the spaghettini bolognese between bowls and serve topped with Sicilian olives, extra chilli flakes and thyme sprigs, a dollop of mascarpone, pepper and Parmigiano Reggiano.

———

Spaghettini was my Nonno Gaetano's favourite pasta with any sauce, but you can use flat noodles like tagliatelle, pappardelle or fettuccine. Nonna Giuseppa knew the faster cooking spaghettini should be paired with a lighter sauce, and Nonno, Jojo and I love the way this pasta scoops up a little more sauce. The background painting is by a dear friend, Regina Newey.

ricotta
and parsley
cannelloni

Fresh tomato sauce 2 (page 30)

Flour and water dough (page 34) or
   store-bought fresh lasagne sheets

90 g (3 oz/1 cup) pecorino, freshly grated

200 g (7 oz) fontina, sliced

ricotta filling

1 kg (2 lb 3 oz/4 cups) smooth ricotta

30 g (1 oz/1 cup) flat-leaf (Italian) parsley,
   finely chopped

2 eggs

pinch of freshly grated nutmeg

sea salt

makes 24 cannelloni

Preheat the oven to 180°C (360°F). Grease two 23 × 30 cm (9 × 12 in) ovenproof dishes with oil.

Make the tomato sauce and set aside. In a large bowl, combine the ricotta, parsley, eggs, nutmeg and season with salt. Set aside.

If using the Flour and water dough, cut the dough into four portions and cover with cling wrap to stop a dry crust forming. With each portion of pasta dough, press down to make a rectangle shape, then use a rolling pin or a pasta machine to roll it out until it is thin and smooth. Cut into 24 squares roughly measuring 130 mm. Set aside, covered, until ready to use.

Spread a cup of tomato sauce over the base of both ovenproof dishes.

Top each square pasta sheet with ¼ cup of the ricotta filling along the centre and roll. Place in a baking dish, seam-side down. Repeat with the remaining pasta sheets and ricotta filling. Spread the remaining tomato mixture over the top of the cannelloni in each dish, and sprinkle with the pecorino and fontina cheese. Cook for 45 minutes, or until golden. Serve as is to the table for guests to help themselves.

—

The winters at Cumbrae were imbued with Western Port Bay winds with layers like ice tissue paper surrounding the farm. By mid-morning the fire was roaring and the moment had arrived to make pasta for ricotta cannelloni. Filled with creamy ricotta and the sweet, grassy, cold freshness of parsley, and bound with the warmth of fresh rasps of nutmeg, this was the dish that made me a cook.

radiatore with peas

125 ml (4 fl oz/½ cup) mild olive oil

2 shallots, finely chopped

1 celery stalk, finely chopped

small handful of finely chopped dill,
plus some small fronds to serve

1 teaspoon chilli flakes (optional),
plus extra to serve

775 g (1 lb 11 oz/5 cups) fresh or frozen peas

2 litres (68 fl oz/8 cups) boiling water

500 g (1 lb 2 oz) radiatore or other short pasta

juice of ½ lemon

salt and freshly ground black pepper

freshly grated pecorino, to serve

enough for 4–6

Heat the oil in a heavy-based saucepan over a medium heat, then add the shallots, celery, dill, chilli (if using), salt and pepper. Fry until the shallots are translucent, about 5–7 minutes. Add 620 g (1 lb 6 oz) of the peas and cook over a low heat for 15 minutes, stirring occasionally. Add the boiling water and season with a pinch of salt. Cook, partially covered, for about 45 minutes. Mash the peas from time to time. By the end the sauce should be a chunky puree.

Bring a large saucepan of water to the boil, add salt and cook the pasta until nearly al dente, then add the remaining peas. Drain the pasta and peas and return them to the pan. Add the lemon juice, season with pepper and stir, then add the pea sauce and stir again.

Serve in individual bowls and top with the extra dill and chilli flakes, if using. Don't forget a big bowl of grated pecorino for the table.

——

Radiatore pasta dressed simply with extra-virgin olive oil and butter, sprinkled with finely grated cheese and lots of pepper, is a favourite that always leaves me wanting more, but radiatore with peas comes a close second. Mushy peas with not-so-mushy peas for the top, finely chopped dill, lemon and a pinch of chilli flakes for a tangy, spiced edge, leaves everyone going back for seconds. My grandbabies' favourite dish is any pasta with peas or pesto (or the two combined). All four of them love it and it's so easy and quick to prepare.

cauliflower and kohlrabi soup

1 cauliflower, trimmed and broken into florets

125 ml (4 fl oz/½ cup) extra-virgin olive oil

2 brown onions, diced

2 leeks, diced

4 carrots, chopped

4 celery stalks, chopped

1 fennel bulb, chopped

handful thyme sprigs, leaves picked,
plus extra thyme sprigs, toasted, to serve

4 kohlrabi, trimmed, peeled and chopped

4 garlic cloves, crushed

2 litres (68 fl oz/8 cups) vegetable or chicken stock

salt and freshly ground black pepper

freshly grated pecorino, to serve

toasted broken bread, dressed with extra-virgin
olive oil and pepper, to serve

enough for 4–6

Preheat the oven to 200°C (390°F).

Toss half of the cauliflower, 2 tablespoons of the oil, and some salt and pepper in a roasting tin and bake for 30 minutes.

Meanwhile, heat the remaining oil in a large saucepan over a medium–high heat. Add the onions and fry, stirring frequently, until translucent, about 5 minutes. Add the leeks, carrots, celery, fennel and thyme and cook a further 5 minutes. Add the remaining cauliflower and the kohlrabi, garlic and stock. Bring to the boil, then reduce the heat to medium, partially cover and simmer until tender, about 45 minutes–1 hour.

Blend the soup using a hand-held blender – chunky or smooth; whichever you prefer. Check the seasoning and adjust if needed.

To serve, ladle the soup into bowls and top with some roasted cauliflower, grated pecorino and broken bread.

—

This irresistible soup is made with all my garden heroes: cauliflower, kohlrabi, fennel, garlic and thyme. Make an extra batch and deliver it to the family next door. Top with toasted thyme sprigs and broken bread as the crowning glory.

—

nonna giuseppa's cauliflower fritters | Cook 800 g (1 lb 12 oz) cauliflower florets in boiling water for 15–20 minutes, until soft, then set aside to cool. Put the florets into a food processor with 4 lightly beaten eggs, 120 g (4½ oz/2 cups) Japanese breadcrumbs, 3 tablespoons finely chopped flat-leaf (Italian) parsley, 2 crushed garlic cloves, 50 g (1¾ oz/½ cup) freshly grated Parmigiano Reggiano, salt and freshly ground black pepper. Process until well mixed. Transfer the mixture to a bowl, cover and rest for 1–2 hours. Use two spoons to roll the mixture into rough quenelles of about 6 cm (2½ in) long. Heat 125 ml (4 fl oz/½ cup) mild olive oil in a large frying over a medium heat. Gently press down on the quenelles as you place them in the pan, then fry for 6–8 minutes on each side, draining on paper towel as you go. Makes 36–40.

jojo's mussels

1.5 kg (3 lb 5 oz) mussels

2 tablespoons mild olive oil

1 small red onion, diced

4 garlic cloves, crushed

400 g (14 oz) tinned finely chopped tomatoes

125 ml (4 fl oz/½ cup) fish stock

60 g (2 oz/2 cups) flat-leaf (Italian) parsley, chopped

salt and freshly ground black pepper

1 long red chilli, trimmed, seeded and julienned, to serve

bruschetta, thickly sliced, to serve (optional)

enough for 4–6

Rinse the mussels under cold running water, scrubbing with a stainless steel scrubbing brush. Grasp the beard and give it a sharp yank, pulling it out. Set the mussels aside in the refrigerator.

Heat the oil in a large frying pan over a medium–high heat, then gently fry the onion and garlic until the onion is soft, about 5 minutes. Add the tomatoes, stock, half of the parsley, salt and pepper and cook gently for 15 minutes, stirring occasionally, until the liquid has reduced a little. Add the mussels and cook over high heat with the lid on until the shells open, about 5 minutes.

Take the pan off the heat and sprinkle with the chilli and the remaining parsley.

Serve immediately with thick slices of bruschetta.

—

Over five decades Johanne and I have criss-crossed the history of our lives together, carrying with it the customs of an ancient land. Since the beginning, a sacred thing has played an integral purpose in how we travel around each other. Sometimes the vibrant pigments of life's incredible journey has brought us smashed colours beyond our wildest dreams, their buoyancy dashed only to cross over from their ancient world to the present day. In the course of a lifetime, the tales of a shoebox filled with faded photographs have delivered decennaries of glamorous windswept smiles, starting with a ridiculously young couple in love enjoying the intoxicating freedom of youth. I keep a small hexagonal glass bottle of this charming history on my bedside table and take a little every morning.

roast pork belly and fennel

1 × 1.5–1.8 kg (3 lb 5 oz–4 lb) boned pork belly, skin on

3 tablespoons extra-virgin olive oil

6 shallots, halved

4 garlic cloves, skins on

3 carrots, chopped

1 celery stalk, chopped

1 fennel bulb, cut into wedges

½ teaspoon chilli flakes

1 teaspoon fennel seeds

1 teaspoon yellow mustard seeds

3 rosemary sprigs

6 thyme sprigs

250 ml (8½ fl oz/1 cup) *Jojo's brodo* (page 21) or chicken stock, plus extra as required

250 ml (8½ fl oz/1 cup) dry marsala

250 ml (8½ fl oz/1 cup) apple-cider vinegar

salt and freshly ground black pepper

enough for 6–8

Preheat the oven to 180°C (360°F).

Cut the pork belly into ten or twelve 3.5–4 cm (1½ in) thick slices or chops.

Heat the oil in a large heavy-based frying pan over a medium heat, then, working in batches, fry the pork pieces on both sides until golden, about 8–10 minutes on each side. This step adds extra flavour.

Spread the fried pork pieces in a large roasting tin. Add the remaining ingredients, cover with aluminium foil and roast for 30 minutes. Remove the foil and roast for another 1½ hours. Make sure the pork has enough liquid while it roasts; if necessary add extra *brodo* or chicken stock to the tin. When ready, the pork should be pull-apart tender, but not mushy. Taste and check the seasoning before serving.

—

Every morning at Cumbrae Farm, a large, heavy pot filled with chunks of pumpkin, vegetable scraps and stale bread from the local baker was heated over a high flame and cooked until the orange porridge was ready to be poured into the pig troughs. I loved watching the pigs at the trough, rubbing against each other, licking and sucking juice off their noses – their snuffling and spirit for foraging was endless. The curious pigs were motivated to explore their large pen and its surroundings, and often managed to escape. There was one pig in particular, who I named Jupiter, with a particularly saintly attitude. I actually saw him levitate over the pen on many occasions and sometimes he even flew to the Monterey cypress, landing on its highest branches while commenting about quince jelly and pumpkin porridge. When Jupiter died, the pigsty lost its always over-thinking, joyous boar with the playful, curious attitude.

pennoni lisci with broken beef brisket

1 × 1.5 kg (3 lb 5 oz) beef brisket

75 g (2¾ oz/½ cup) plain (all-purpose) flour seasoned with salt and freshly ground black pepper

3 tablespoons mild olive oil

1 litre (34 fl oz/4 cups) beef stock

500 ml (17 fl oz/2 cups) red wine

¼ teaspoon sichuan peppercorns

4 cloves

4 star anise

4 cardamom pods

1 cinnamon stick

1 tablespoon coriander seeds

4 thick slices fresh ginger, skin on

1 bay leaf

3 thyme sprigs

400 g (14 oz) pennoni lisci

freshly grated Parmigiano Reggiano, to serve

spiced sofrito

1 brown onion, diced

1 carrot, diced

1 celery stalk with leaves, diced

4 garlic cloves, chopped

¼ teaspoon dried chilli flakes

¼ teaspoon fennel seeds

enough for 4

Preheat the oven to 170°C (340°F).

Wash the brisket and pat it dry with paper towel. Trim off any excess fat and cut the brisket into four pieces. Roll the beef in the seasoned flour and shake off any excess. Heat the oil a large enamelled cast-iron casserole pot over a medium–high heat and sear the brisket on all sides until golden brown.

Turn the heat down to medium, add the spiced sofrito ingredients, nuzzling it in and around the brisket. Gently cook for about 2 minutes. Remove the pot from the heat, then add the stock, wine and all of the spices and herbs. Cover the pot and transfer to the oven to cook for 4 hours. (Alternatively, continue to cook it on the stovetop over a low heat for the same amount of time.)

When it is ready, it's time to shred the brisket. Remove the brisket from the pot and use two forks to shred it apart. Return the shredded brisket to the pot and keep it warm on the stovetop while you prepare the pasta.

Bring a large saucepan of water to the boil, add salt and cook the pennoni lisci until just before al dente. Add the pasta to the pot with the brisket and stir. Cover and rest for a few minutes.

To serve, divide between bowls. Don't forget to offer a big bowl of freshly grated Parmigiano Reggiano for everyone to help themselves.

—

Today I tested this recipe for the book again. It reminded me how powerful memories of cooking can be. The effect they have on our emotions, simmering away like our dreams to discover many essential bits of ourselves. Yesterday marked almost 65 years since our arrival to the farm. Cumbrae Farm is long gone now but its voice is suspended in time.

spiced chicken

3 tablespoons extra-virgin olive oil

12 boneless, skinless chicken thighs

6 chicken legs

250 ml (8½ fl oz/1 cup) white wine

6 garlic cloves, skins on, crushed

2 walnut-sized pieces of fresh ginger, sliced

1 teaspoon chilli flakes

4–5 rosemary sprigs, plus extra to serve

1 teaspoon fennel seeds

1 tablespoon ground coriander

1 tablespoon ground cumin

1 teaspoon ground turmeric

3 star anise

3 cloves

2 cardamon pods

1 teaspoon smoked paprika

1 cinnamon stick

3 tablespoons tomato paste (concentrated puree)

2 litres (68 fl oz/8 cups) *Jojo's brodo* (page 21) or chicken stock

4 zucchini (courgette), chopped into diamonds

200 g (7 oz/1 cup) Sicilian olives

salt and freshly ground black pepper

parsley sprigs, to serve (optional)

couscous

370 g (13 oz/2 cups) couscous

500 ml (17 fl oz/2 cups) boiling *Jojo's brodo* (page 21), chicken stock or water

2 tablespoons finely chopped flat-leaf (Italian) parsley or mint (optional)

80 g (3 oz/½ cup) pine nuts, toasted with ¼ teaspoon cumin and ¼ teaspoon smoked paprika (optional)

enough for 6–12

Heat the oil in a large heavy-based saucepan over a medium–high heat, then fry the chicken in batches until golden on both sides, about 8–10 minutes, then set aside. Deglaze the pan with the wine, scraping all the lovely bits from the bottom of the pan. Add the garlic, ginger, chilli flakes, rosemary, fennel seeds, ground coriander, cumin, turmeric, star anise, cloves, cardamon, paprika, cinnamon and tomato paste. Give it a good stir – the liquid will be a gorgeous deep orange-red. Return the chicken to the pan, add the *brodo* and bring to the boil. Reduce the heat to low, then simmer, covered, for about 20 minutes. Remove the lid and simmer for another 20 minutes. Check the seasoning, add the zucchini and cook for 5 minutes more. Remove the pan from the heat and stir through the olives.

To make the couscous, combine the couscous in a large bowl with the boiling *brodo* and stir vigorously to combine. Cover immediately with a tight lid or cling wrap to allow the couscous to absorb all the liquid. After 5 minutes, fluff the couscous up with a fork, gently scraping across the top layer, then turn 45 degrees and fluff up the second layer. Repeat until you get to the bottom of the bowl. Mix through the herbs and toasted, seasoned pine nuts or leave it plain if you prefer.

Serve the chicken with extra rosemary sprigs and parsley (if using) with the couscous on the side in a bowl.

—

Sicily has been conquered by nearly everyone, including Italy in 1860. Of all the island's invaders, it's Tunisia, Algeria and Morocco that have had the most influence on the cuisine, bringing couscous, oranges, lemons, artichokes, rice, almonds, pistachios and spices, such as cinnamon, saffron, sumac, nutmeg, cloves, sesame and dried fruits.

chicken with cauliflower and pearl couscous

200 g (7 oz) cauliflower, broken into florets

2 long thin eggplants (aubergines), trimmed and cut into discs

80 ml (2½ fl oz/⅓ cup) extra-virgin olive oil, plus extra to drizzle

1 teaspoon smoked paprika

1 teaspoon ground cumin

200 g (7 oz) cabbage

1 baby cos (romaine) lettuce, quartered, then halved

200 g (7 oz/1 cup) quinoa, cooked

75 g (2¾ oz/½ cup) pearl couscous, cooked

leftover *Jojo's brodo* (page 21) or roast chicken, shredded

100 g (3½ oz) soft goat's cheese

salt

1 handful of dill tops, to serve

1 handful of borage tops with flowers or the tops of mint or some watercress or young pea shoots, to serve

enough for 4–6

Preheat the oven to 200°C (390°F).

Toss the cauliflower and eggplant together with the oil, paprika and cumin in a large bowl. Season with salt, then spread out in a single layer on a baking tray. Roast for 20–30 minutes, or until golden. Remove from the oven and allow to cool.

Put the cooled cauliflower and eggplant into a large bowl. Cut the core from the cabbage and remove any ragged outer leaves, then slice the leaves crossways as thinly as you can. Add the cabbage to the bowl with the cauliflower and eggplant. Add the cos lettuce, quinoa, couscous, chicken, goat's cheese and very gently toss.

To serve, transfer to a serving dish, drizzle with extra oil and scatter the herbs on top. This would be lovely with a side of rinsed crisp radishes with their leafy tops.

—

Any leftover *brodo* chicken or roast chicken is terrific tossed through pasta, in a pot pie with mushrooms or with a salad. It also makes an excellent sandwich with capers, celery, toasted pine nuts and cos leaves, drizzled with olive oil and lemon.

The voice of the cypress is always in my pocket, ever since that first night I slept under its branches. Many years later, in Sicily, I entered an abandoned house right in the centre of a village. Like the sheds at Cumbrae Farm, the furniture left behind was covered in mournful layers of dust while voices of ghosts hovered in shadowy corners. One room was painted in cyclamen pink and had green and red clouds running across the Brutesco-style ceiling and faded frescoes of Byzantine gods representing centuries of overindulgence and excess.

Foreigners who visited were greeted in another room with elaborate, stained burgundy curtains, like fragments of verses dipped in sauce piquant. The walls were lined with shelves of first-edition books – Rudyard Kipling, Charles Dickens, Arthur Conan Doyle, Oscar Wilde. My hand rippled against elaborate enamelled plaques attached by silk in blue and gold ribbons.

This room took me high into the branches of the cypress to reach my grandbabies, who had climbed through its scaly trunk, slashed with deep cuts, crawling their way up to the crown. Raphael, Theodore, Otto and Leni are drenched in its deep-green feathery clouds, exchanging gossip with bells of laughter. The cypress is so beautiful: it comes alive again whenever I take it out of my pocket.

giuseppe's confit duck

8 duck legs

1 tablespoon juniper berries

8 star anise

1 tablespoon black peppercorns

2 cinnamon sticks

1 teaspoon cloves

3 cardamon pods

6 thyme sprigs

4 bay leaves

90 g (30 oz/⅔ cup) salt flakes

500 g (1 lb 2 oz) duck fat

olive oil, if required

sliced pancetta, to serve (optional)

grated pecorino cheese, to serve (optional)

chilli flakes, to serve (optional)

freshly ground pepper, to server (optional)

enough for 8

Wash the duck legs under cold running water and pat them dry with paper towel.

Combine the juniper berries, star anise, peppercorns, cinnamon, cloves and cardamon with three of the thyme sprigs and two of the bay leaves in a bowl. Sprinkle half of the herb mix on the bottom of a large roasting tin and lay the duck legs on top, skin side up. Sprinkle the remaining herb mix on top and sprinkle with the salt flakes. Cover and refrigerate at least for 6 hours, or up to 24 hours if you prefer a saltier duck.

Preheat the oven to 140°C (285°F). Wash the duck legs again under cold running water and pat dry.

Warm 2 tablespoons of the duck fat in a heavy-based frying pan over medium–high heat, then lightly brown the duck legs on both sides, about 8–10 minutes. Place the duck legs in a clean roasting tin, skin side up. Heat the remaining duck fat until it turns to liquid, then pour it over the duck legs. Add the remaining thyme and bay leaves. If required, top up with olive oil so that the duck is just covered. Roast for 2½ hours to confit. The duck is ready when the meat starts to pull away from the bone. Drain the duck legs, place on a baking tray and refrigerate for 2 hours.

Preheat the oven to 200°C (390°F) and line a clean roasting tin with baking paper.

Remove the fat from the duck legs and place them, skin side down, in the prepared tin. Roast for 15–20 minutes, turning halfway. The duck is ready when it's warm and the skin is crisp. If serving with crisp pancetta, spread some pancetta on a baking tray and cook in the oven with the duck legs until crisp, about 12–15 minutes. Garnish with pecorino cheese, chilli flakes and freshly ground pepper, if desired.

—

This rich duck confit, developed by Giuseppe Trinci, is one of my favourite dishes. When I worked with Joe in the cafe, we served duck confit with roast potatoes and a shaved fennel salad, or sometimes with some crisp pancetta. Alternatively, you can serve confit duck with fettuccine flavoured with butter, orange zest, dill sprigs and any pan juices from the pancetta and duck (as pictured). Don't forget the just-blanched peas quickly tossed in a hot frying pan with a little olive oil and butter.

vodka and strawberry gluten-free cake | Preheat the oven to 180°C (360°F). Grease and line a 32.5 cm (12¾ in) round cake tin, 7.5 cm (3 in) deep, with butter and line with baking paper. Combine 500 ml (17 fl oz/2 cups) sunflower oil, 4 eggs, the grated zest and juice of 1 orange, 2 tablespoons vodka, 250 g (9 oz/1 cup) mascarpone and 575 g (1 lb 4 oz/2½ cups) caster sugar in a large bowl and whisk to combine. Sift together 450 g (1 lb/3 cups) gluten-free self-raising flour and 185 g (6½ oz/1½ cups) cornflour (cornstarch) in a separate bowl, then gently fold the flours and 100 g (3½ oz) halved strawberries into the wet mixture until just combined. Pour the batter into the prepared tin and bake for 50–55 minutes, or until it tests done with a skewer. Cool in the tin for 15 minutes, then turn out onto a wire rack to cool completely. Serve with 100 g (3½ oz) strawberries and thick (double/heavy) cream, Greek-style yoghurt or mascarpone whipped with a touch of vodka and orange zest. Enough for 12–15.

olive oil, citrus and honey cake

300 g (10½ oz/2 cups) self-raising flour

220 g (8 oz/1 cup) caster sugar

45 g (1½ oz/¼ cup) soft brown sugar

½ teaspoon bicarbonate of soda (baking soda)

pinch of salt

4 eggs

185 ml (6 fl oz/¾ cup) extra-virgin olive oil

3 tablespoons honey

grated zest of 2 oranges

grated zest of 1 lemon

honey mascarpone

330 g (11½ oz/1½ cups) mascarpone mixed with 2 tablespoons honey (optional)

enough for 8–10 people

Preheat the oven to 180°C (360°F). Spray a 24 cm (9 in) round non-stick springform tin with oil and line the base and side with baking paper.

Sift the flour, both sugars, bicarbonate of soda and salt into a large bowl and combine well. In another bowl, use a balloon whisk to combine the eggs, oil, honey and orange and lemon zest. Make a well in the centre of the dry ingredients, then pour in the wet. Stir until just combined.

Pour into a prepared tin and bake for 35–40 minutes, or until it tests done with a skewer or springs back to the touch. Let the cake cool a little in the tin before releasing it from the tin and transferring to a serving plate.

Served warm, this cake is perfect on its own with tea or coffee or accompanied by a generous dollop of honey mascarpone.

This cake will keep for up to 3 days stored in an airtight container in the refrigerator (bring to room temperature or warm through before serving).

——

Olive oil cake has so much to offer – it justly deserves to be everywhere. The hit of citrus in this cake cleanses the soul, then the taste of honey makes me want to sin again. Olive oil cake has no elaborate curtains to hide behind and doesn't need improvements of any kind.

IT'S INSPIRING

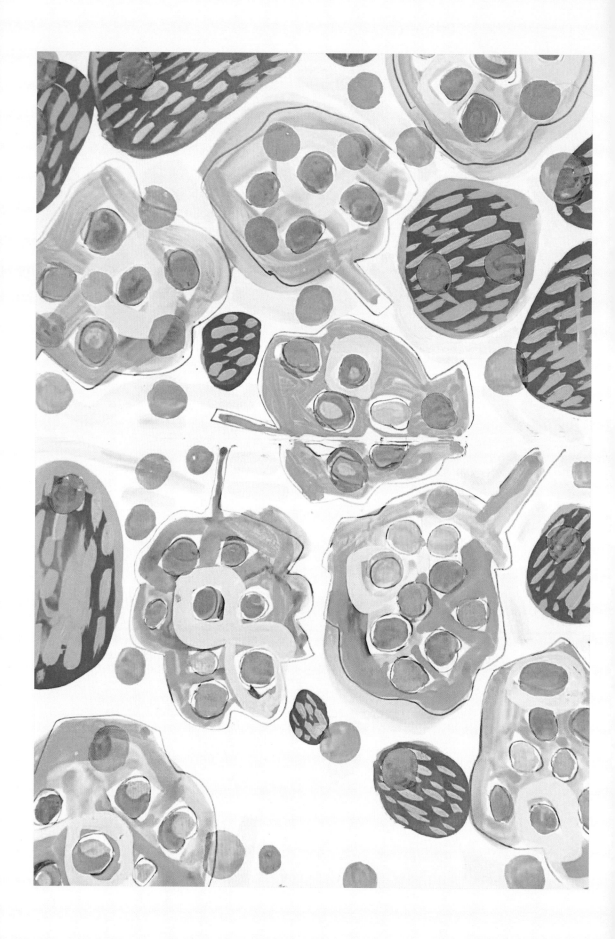

Dear Raphael, Theodore, Otto and Leni, spring is my favourite season. The most exquisite delicacies are those the comet spirits found beneath the stars and rays of the moon. With arms linked between Mars and Jupiter, I wait for the still moments to save its drops to give to you. For every second of every day.

Spring is statues of marbled angels with gossamer wings wearing Japanese silk that shimmers in the light; twenty-one, twenty-two, twenty-three, twenty-four silver horses, flying past at a 5:55 am sunrise.

Spring is the act of applying dark cherry-red lipstick as the finishing touch to a fully made-up face for added oomph, captured in frosted glass that is edged in gold dust from asteroid 16 Psyche – the cosmic energy between the orbits of Jupiter and Mars.

The thirty days of November have finally squeezed through the bush at the edge of the farm – our first spring was coming to an end. I follow twenty-five, twenty-six, twenty-seven stallions, mares and foals to the end of McKirdys Road, turning left into Denhams Road for Western Port Bay. I pass through the dead branches of the weeping willow in old Mrs Denham's front garden – low enough to break, snap and make a bow, cutting a notch at either end for the string, bending the wood just enough to pull back an arrow. Running up the hill through the sea scrub towards the small beach, I finally trudge through the marshy waters with small, pale yellowish to greenish poisonous toadfish (*Tetractenos glaber*). They are spotty and blotchy, with dark tiger bands on their backs, craving dense sea grasses to hide. They are quick to disappear under the few little boats tethered to aged wooden posts. They are at the mercy of the rhythm of the last moon's tide.

Spring mornings are the best. Floating face-down, fully dressed in the unruly water. The sensuality of the bay: fish talk among chocolate mangroves that lay like saint's relics, guarding squadrons of crabs in Valencia orange, dressed like popes from the Venetian Renaissance.

Delicious little handmade books with patterns in vivid colours rest on a chocolatey embroidered tablecloth among the ordered chaos of the kitchen. Discarded fish heads on blue-lined graph paper are left in bowls beside bottles of homemade wine and large, simmering pots of tomato sugo in battered steel saucepans. Plastic green templates of Australia jostle for space among set squares; parchment paper is scattered everywhere, covered with coloured crayon; chalky seashells in fleeting shades of copper, sandy greys and whites mingle with common garden snails gathered after the first of the spring rains to serve one month later in potato and garlic soup.

All of my reading books had the capital letters T, O and M scrawled in stick-figure handwriting on the inside covers. Sometimes the letters were in alternating colours of yellow, red and cobalt blue with touches of emerald green zig-zag lines framing the characters. Magpie practises yoga, stretching his wings, bending and twirling, issuing screeching orders to the blessed pink-and-orange striped squid caught on the end of squid jiggers floating outside my bedroom window.

fresh radish with pomegranate and bacon | Thoroughly wash 16 fresh radishes with their stems, leaves and root tips intact under cold running water. Sprinkle the radishes with 1 teaspoon smoked paprika, then set aside. Place 8 streaky bacon rashers (slices) in a single layer in a non-stick frying pan over a medium heat. Fry for 10–15 minutes, then turn and fry for another 5 minutes, or until golden. Meanwhile, toast 8 thick slices of sourdough baguette or ciabatta, then rub one side with a peeled and cut garlic clove. Place the toast on a serving dish and drizzle with a little extra-virgin olive oil. Top with the bacon and scatter 3 tablespoons pomegranate seeds over the top. Serve with the radishes on the side. Enough for 4.

artichoke omelette | Trim the stems of 2 artichokes to about 1 cm (½ in), then cut the remaining long stems in half lengthways. Tear the outer leaves off each artichoke until you reach the inner pale, tender leaves. Slice 2–3 cm (¾–1¼ in) off the top of the cone (depending on the size), then use the point of a knife to remove the fury 'choke' from inside. Cut each artichoke into quarters, then rub the quarters and stem pieces all over with a cut lemon. Cook the artichokes in salted boiling water over a medium heat until tender, about 10 minutes. Heat 3 tablespoons mild olive oil in a large frying pan over a medium heat, then add 4 unpeeled shallots and the artichokes and cook for another 10 minutes. Meanwhile, in a bowl combine 6 beaten eggs with 125 ml (4 fl oz/½ cup) pouring (single/light) cream and 25 g (1 oz/¼ cup) freshly grated pecorino and season with salt and freshly ground black pepper. Pour the eggs into the frying pan over the artichokes. Crumble 75 g (2¾ oz/½ cup) soft goat's cheese over the top. As the omelette starts to cook, use a spatula to gently pull the egg back from the side of the pan, folding to break the omelette over on itself. Add a small handful of chopped flat-leaf (Italian) parsley and watercress to serve. Enough for 2–3.

Pasta cu fave is made with fresh broad (fava) beans, or with dried beans when not in season (page 112). Without the pasta, the fresh and cheerful thick soup is especially good served with crusty oven-roasted bread and a chunk of pecorino, topped with thick-cut pancetta and heaps of chopped dill.

orecchiette with fresh broad beans | Heat 2 tablespoons extra-virgin olive oil in a saucepan over a medium heat, then add 350 g (12½ oz) shelled and peeled broad (fava) beans and 1 finely chopped shallot. Season with salt and freshly ground black pepper and fry for about 15 minutes, stirring occasionally, until the beans start to break down and change colour. Add 500 ml (17 fl oz/2 cups) of boiling water and continue to cook, partially covered, for 30 minutes, mashing the beans a little during this time. Meanwhile, bring a large saucepan of water to the boil, add salt and cook 350 g (12½ oz) orecchiette until just before al dente. Drain the pasta, reserving 125 ml (4 fl oz/½ cup) of the pasta water. Pour the pasta and pasta water into the broad bean sauce, then rest with the lid on for 2 minutes before serving topped with 2–3 heaped tablespoons roasted, thick-cut pancetta, a scattering of finely chopped fresh dill and freshly grated ricotta salata or 2–3 tablespoons fresh ricotta. Season with more pepper and serve with a lemon half. Enough for 4.

broad bean pesto with whatever pasta takes your weeknight mood | For a fast weeknight fresh broad (fava) bean pasta, boil 350 g (12½ oz) shelled and peeled broad beans for about 5 minutes, or until tender. Drain, reserving 250 ml (8½ fl oz/1 cup) of the water, and run the broad beans under cold running water. Put aside 185 g (6½ oz/1 cup) of the broad beans and place the rest into the bowl of a food processor. Blend with 45 g (1½ oz/1 cup) baby English spinach leaves, 6–8 basil leaves and a similar quantity of dill and flat-leaf (Italian) parsley until it reaches a rough texture. Season with salt and freshly ground black pepper. Pour in 125 ml (4 fl oz/½ cup) extra-virgin olive oil and pulse to a smooth pesto. If it is too thick, add a little of the reserved broad bean water. Bring a large saucepan of water to the boil, add salt and cook 350 g (12½ oz) of whatever pasta takes your weeknight mood until al dente. Drain, then return the pasta to the pot. Add the broad bean sauce and toss. Serve topped with the reserved broad beans, a scattering of thinly sliced green chilli and 2–3 tablespoons *Pangrattato* (page 26). Enough for 4.

linguine with broad beans, peas, silverbeet and mascarpone

120 ml (4 fl oz) extra-virgin olive oil

50 g (1¾ oz) salted butter

1 leek, thinly sliced

200 g (7 oz/1 cup) mascarpone

400 g (14 oz) linguine

1 kg (2 lb 3 oz) broad (fava) beans, shelled

200 g (7 oz) green beans, sliced lengthways

500 g (1 lb 2 oz) fresh peas in their pods or 200 g (7 oz) frozen peas

4 silverbeet (Swiss chard) leaves, stems removed and leaves torn

salt and freshly ground black pepper

enough for 4

Heat the olive oil and butter in a large heavy-based frying pan over a low–medium heat and add the leek. Fry for 8–10 minutes, or until soft. Add the mascarpone and some salt and pepper and gently stir to heat through. Turn the heat off.

Meanwhile, bring a large saucepan of water to the boil, add salt and cook the linguine with the broad beans, green beans, peas and silverbeet until the pasta is al dente. Drain the linguine and vegetables, leaving a little water in the pan. Pour the pasta and vegetables into the pan with the leek and mascarpone sauce and gently fold to combine.

To serve, divide between plates.

—

Love and pain and the whole Sicilian broad bean thing. The amount of broad beans to be found in a Sicilian garden should not be underestimated. We always grow far too many. Mine grow in among the flowers in my front garden. Every available space has seeds pushed into the dirt, eventually filling the gap with beautiful shrubs. They give the greatest joy when the flowers appear, then the slender pods with the first of the sweet beans can be picked and eaten raw. And before you know it they have burst into long, spectacular, erect clusters of pods.

lamb with eggplant

80 ml (2½ fl oz/⅓ cup) extra-virgin olive oil

250 g (9 oz) shallots, peeled

4–5 garlic bulbs, whole, skins on

2 celery stalks, chopped

2 fennel bulbs, chopped

4 thyme sprigs

2 bay leaves

4 rosemary sprigs

1 × 2 kg (4 lb 6 oz) lamb shoulder with the bone in

salt and freshly ground black pepper

date dressing

100 g (3½ oz) pitted dates

375 ml (12½ fl oz/1½ cups) whisky

1 garlic clove, crushed

juice of 1 lemon

spice mix

1 teaspoon fennel seeds

1 teaspoon ground cumin

1 teaspoon chilli flakes

tzatziki (optional)

2 telegraph (long) cucumbers, cut into thick chunks

250 g (9 oz/1 cup) Greek-style yoghurt, strained

1 garlic clove, grated

grated zest and juice of 1 lemon

handful of torn mint leaves

3–4 dill sprigs, chopped, to taste

good pinch of salt

1 tablespoon extra-virgin olive oil

eggplant

2 eggplants (aubergines), chopped

1 teaspoon salt

125 ml (4 fl oz/½ cup) mild olive oil

enough for 6–8

Preheat the oven to 180°C (360°F). Grease a large roasting tin with oil and line with baking paper.

For the date dressing, soak the dates in 125 ml (4 fl oz/½ cup) of the whisky for at least 15 minutes and set aside. To make the spice mix, combine the spices in a small bowl and set aside. If making the tzatziki, combine the ingredients in a bowl and mix.

Pour the extra-virgin olive oil into the roasting tin, and add some of the shallots, garlic, celery and fennel with some of the herbs. Place the lamb on top, then add the rest of the shallots, garlic, celery, fennel, herbs and the spice mix on top of and around the lamb. Season with salt and pepper, cover with aluminium foil and cook for 2½ hours. Remove the foil and cook for 1 hour more. Start prepping the eggplant 30–40 minutes before the lamb will be ready to come out of the oven. When ready, remove the lamb from the oven and rest, covered, for 20–30 minutes.

To make the spiced eggplant, put the eggplant in a large bowl with the salt and mix well. Set aside for 30 minutes. Tip the eggplant out onto a baking tray and pat dry with paper towel. Wipe out the bowl, then tip the eggplant back in and drizzle with the olive oil. Mix well. Spread out into a large roasting tin and roast for 30 minutes, stirring after 15 minutes, until golden brown. Place into a serving dish and set aside.

Meanwhile, make the date dressing by gently heating the date mixture and remaining whisky with the garlic and lemon juice in a small saucepan over low heat until the liquid has reduced, around 8–10 minutes. Set aside to cool. Once cool, spoon it over the eggplant.

I like to serve the lamb in the roasting tin, keeping everything looking lovely and rustic. Serve the eggplant on the side with some tzatziki (if using).

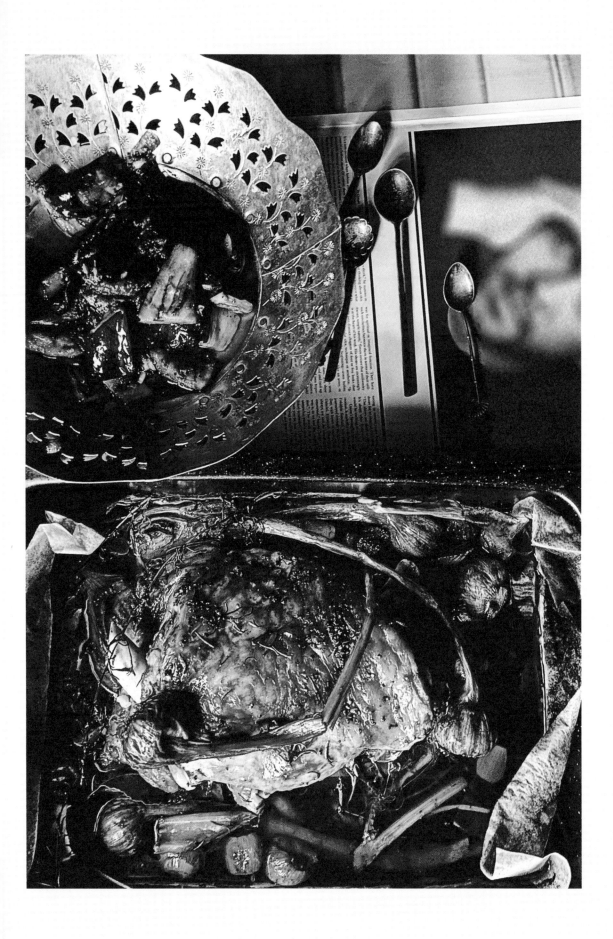

lamb shanks

3 tablespoons mild olive oil

4 lamb shanks, washed and patted dry

3 shallots, chopped

1 celery stalk, chopped

2 carrots, chopped

8 garlic cloves, skins on

70 g (2½ oz/16 fillets) anchovy fillets
   (I use the little ones in a jar)

90 g (3 oz/⅓ cup) tomato paste (concentrated puree)

6 thyme sprigs

6 rosemary sprigs

500 ml (17 fl oz/2 cups) dry marsala

750 ml (25½ fl oz/3 cups) dry red wine

salt and freshly ground black pepper

enough for 4

Preheat the oven to 180°C (360°F).

Heat the oil in a large enamelled cast-iron casserole pot over a medium–high heat, then fry the shanks until golden all over, about 8–10 minutes. Turn down the heat, add the shallot, celery, carrot, garlic and anchovies (do not skimp, trust me) and stir for 2–3 minutes. Add the tomato paste and herbs and stir for another 2–3 minutes. Add the marsala and red wine and stir the shanks around so the liquid is well mixed. Cover and continue to cook in the oven for 2½–3 hours. After 1 hour, turn the shanks over and check the seasoning.

To serve, divide the shanks between plates and, if you like, serve with some mashed potatoes and crusty bread to mop it all up.

—

You don't really need to do much prep or fuss around with side dishes when you cook these lamb shanks. It's the type of meal where all you need is your favourite mashed or crushed potatoes, a good crusty white sourdough bread and a smile.

In the spring evenings at Cumbrae Farm, when the late sun was calling us home, we'd race back through the paperbarks to the kitchen. It was the very best place to be after a day of exploring: barefoot with salty, sun-kissed skin, inhaling the aroma of slow-cooked lamb shanks.

chargrilled lamb salad | Bring 2 lamb backstraps to room temperature on a large plate. Combine 3 tablespoons extra-virgin olive oil, 2 grated garlic cloves, 1 tablespoon dried oregano, salt and freshly ground black pepper in a bowl. Pour the herby oil over the lamb, rubbing it all over and massaging the meat. Heat a barbecue grill or chargrill pan over medium–high until hot. Grill the lamb for 3–4 minutes on each side for medium, or until cooked to your liking. Remove from the heat and transfer to a board to rest, loosely covered with aluminium foil, for 10 minutes. Meanwhile, combine 155 g (5½ oz) fresh, blanched peas, 2 small thinly sliced zucchini (courgette), 8 radicchio leaves of various sizes, 140 g (5 oz/1 cup) crumbled marinated goat's cheese, 160 g (5½ oz/1 cup) edamame beans blanched for 2–3 minutes, then refreshed under cold water and 20 g (¾ oz/1 cup) each of mint, flat-leaf (Italian) parsley and dill in a large bowl. Add the lamb and toss the salad two or three times. Do not overmix – keep some clumps of various ingredients together. Serve on a large dish. Enough for 4.

creamy chicken with roasted beetroot | Preheat the oven to 180°C (360°F). Season 6 chicken thigh fillets with salt and freshly ground black pepper. Heat 3 tablespoons mild olive oil in an enamelled cast-iron casserole pot over medium–high heat, then fry the chicken, skin side down, on both sides until golden brown, about 8–10 minutes. Remove the chicken from the pan and set aside. Turn the heat down to medium and fry 6 halved field mushrooms for 2 minutes on each side. Pour in 2 tablespoons red-wine vinegar, 3 halved shallots, 6 peeled, whole garlic cloves, 2 bay leaves and 125 ml (4 fl oz/½ cup) each of dry white wine and dry marsala or sherry. Cook for another 7 minutes, or until slightly thickened. Add 40 g (1½ oz) salted butter and stir to mix well. Add the chicken back in, skin side up, then pour in 300 ml (10 fl oz/1¼ cups) thick (double/heavy) cream, 1 tablespoon grainy mustard, 2 tarragon sprigs and check the seasoning. Transfer the pot to the oven and cook for 30–40 minutes. Meanwhile, put 12 rinsed and trimmed baby beetroot (beets) into a baking dish with 2 tablespoons olive oil and season. Roast for 30–40 minutes. Rest the chicken for about 10 minutes, keeping it warm under aluminium foil, then serve with the roasted beetroots and toasted, flaked almonds on the top. Enough for 6.

pork rind bruciuluni with pork belly ragu

1 × 1.5–1.7 kg (3 lb 5–3 lb 12 oz)
   boned pork belly, rind on

pork rind stuffing

6 slices of thick-cut, day-old white bread,
   crusts removed and torn into large pieces
   (makes about 2 cups)

90 g (3 oz/1 cup) pecorino, freshly grated

100 g (3½ oz) provolone dolce, torn

2 garlic cloves, sliced

10 g (¼ oz/½ cup) flat-leaf (Italian) parsley, chopped

1 tablespoon rosemary leaves, chopped

2 eggs

1 tablespoon extra-virgin olive oil

salt and freshly ground black pepper

ragu

3 tablespoons extra-virgin olive oil

1 brown onion, diced

1 carrot, diced

1 celery stalk, diced

3 garlic cloves, skins on, crushed

¼ teaspoon chilli flakes

1 teaspoon fennel seeds

500 ml (17 fl oz/2 cups) red wine

2 × 400 g (14 oz) tinned chopped tomatoes

2 bay leaves

small handful of thyme sprigs

salt and freshly ground black pepper

fresh rosemary sprigs, to garnish

enough for 4–6

To stuff the rind, lay the pork belly flat on a board with the rind facing up. Cut the rind away from the meat. Cut the meat into large chunks and set aside. Turn the rind over and lay it flat on the bench.

In a food processor, combine the stuffing ingredients and pulse to mix well. Starting from the widest side, spread the stuffing evenly on top of the pork rind, cut side up, then fold it over and roll the rind up, securing it with a piece of kitchen twine and set aside.

To make the ragu, heat the oil in a large saucepan over medium heat, add the pork belly meat and brown it all over. Remove the meat from the pan and set aside. Place the stuffed rind pieces into the pan and lightly brown all over, gently turning as it's browning. Set aside. Reduce to a low heat, add the onion, carrot and celery to the pan and gently fry until the onion is translucent, about 7–8 minutes. Stir in the garlic, chilli flakes and fennel seeds and cook for another 3 minutes. Return the pork belly meat and rind to the pan, pour in the wine and add the tomatoes with a tin of water. Add the herbs, season and bring to the boil. Reduce the heat to very low and simmer for 3½–4 hours.

Spoon the ragu into serving dishes, then cut the stuffed pork rind into four to six thick slices and place to one side of the ragu. Garnish with rosemary.

———

Cumbrae Farm was a lifetime ago and yet it seems only yesterday its kitchen provided a steady stream of *cucina povera* (peasant cooking). The ingenuity of stuffed pork rind speaks volumes, it was the heart and soul of the Cumbrae kitchen. The long, slow cooking develops a unique texture and flavour. The best part: mopping up the ragu and melting pork rind with chunks of pasta dura.

crumbed sardines with chickpeas

8 slices pancetta

12 whole sardines

75 g (2¾ oz/½ cup) plain (all-purpose) flour

pinch of salt

3 eggs

180 g (6½ oz/3 cups) Japanese breadcrumbs

grated zest of 1 lemon

45 g (1½ oz) pecorino, freshly grated

15 g (½ oz/½ cup) finely chopped flat-leaf (Italian) parsley

1 garlic clove, crushed

mild olive, canola or grape seed oil, for frying

tomato and chickpea sauce

3 tablespoons extra-virgin olive oil

2 shallots, finely chopped

5 wild fennel fronds or dill sprigs

6 garlic cloves, skins on

1 teaspoon chilli flakes

1 teaspoon white (granulated) sugar

400 g (14 oz) tinned chopped tomatoes, put through a mouli

400 g (14 oz) tinned chickpeas

155 g (5½ oz/1 cup) fresh or frozen peas

salt and freshly ground black pepper

enough for 4

Fry the pancetta in a large, dry frying pan over a medium–high heat until crisp, about 4–5 minutes. Set aside.

To make the sauce, heat the extra-virgin olive oil in a heavy-based frying pan over medium heat, then fry the shallots until they are soft, about 8–10 minutes. Add the fennel and continue to cook gently until the aroma fills the kitchen. Add the garlic, chilli flakes, sugar and tomatoes. Fill the tomato tin with water and add this to the saucepan, then add the tinned chickpeas including the chickpea water. Stir and check the seasoning. Bring to the boil, then reduce the heat to low and simmer for 15–20 minutes. Add the peas and cook for 5 minutes longer.

Meanwhile, clean the sardines by removing the heads and tails (or leave them on if you prefer). Run your thumb down the belly of the sardine towards the tail, removing the innards as you go. Remove the fins and all the spiny bits. Open the sardine up and carefully pull away the backbone. Rinse the butterflied sardines under cold running water, drain on paper towel and set aside.

Combine the flour and salt on a large plate. Lightly whisk the eggs in a shallow dish. In a separate dish, combine the breadcrumbs, lemon zest, pecorino, parsley and garlic and season with salt.

Lightly coat the sardines in the flour, shaking off any excess, then dip them into the egg, then the breadcrumb mixture. You may need to gently press the breadcrumbs onto the sardines with your fingertips to coat them.

Add oil to a depth of 5 mm (¼ in) in a large frying pan. Heat over medium–high heat, then fry the sardines in batches until golden and just cooked through, about 2 minutes on each side.

Serve the sardines with the crisp pancetta and the tomato and chickpea sauce.

clam soup with the fish that almost got away

4 garlic cloves, chopped

30 g (1 oz/1 cup) chopped flat-leaf (Italian) parsley leaves

pinch of salt

3 tablespoons extra-virgin olive oil, plus extra to drizzle

1 tablespoon tomato paste (concentrated puree)

1 teaspoon chilli flakes, plus extra to serve

1 teaspoon fennel seeds, crushed

4 silverbeet (Swiss chard) leaves, tender tops only, chopped

3 × 200 g (7 oz) firm, white fish fillets (such as striped trumpeter, rockling or blue-eye trevally), skins off, chopped into bite-sized pieces

750 g (1 lb 11 oz) clams (vongole), washed under cold water

salt and freshly ground black pepper

crusty bread, to serve

enough for 6–8

In a mortar, pound the garlic, parsley and a pinch of salt until it forms a paste.

Heat the oil in a large saucepan over a low heat, then add the garlic paste, tomato paste, chilli flakes and fennel seeds and fry until it becomes a light golden colour, about 2–3 minutes. Add 2 litres (68 fl oz/8 cups) of water and bring to the boil, then reduce the heat to low and simmer for 20 minutes. Add the silverbeet, fish and clams and cook over high heat with the lid on until the shells open, about 5 minutes. Season to taste.

Transfer the soup to a deep serving dish, drizzle with extra oil, sprinkle with extra chilli flakes and serve with crusty bread.

———

Nonna's *brodu cu lu pisci scappatu* (soup with the fish that got away) was cooked for a large family with the only ingredients being water and a heap of garlic and parsley with pastina. Sometimes she added tomato paste and chopped bitter greens. I really want you to have the experience of cooking this beautifully simple broth. I can think of countless other ingredients to celebrate Nonna's *brodo* (broth) with the fish that got away – adding a few mussels, prawns (shrimp), squid, even some mushrooms like shiitake, oyster or any of those curious fungi you might find at the mushroom stall at your local farmers' market.

pickled cucumbers, quinoa, black rice and raw baby carrots

200 g (7 oz/1 cup) quinoa

200 g (7 oz/1 cup) black rice

pinch of salt

1 tablespoon extra-virgin olive oil

1 bunch baby carrots including the green leafy tops

1 zucchini (courgette), sliced into thin discs

200 g (7 oz) green beans, tops trimmed, blanched

salt and freshly ground black pepper

pickled cucumbers

250 ml (8½ fl oz/1 cup) apple-cider vinegar

230 g (8 oz/1 cup) caster sugar

1 teaspoon black mustard seeds

1 teaspoon green peppercorns

1 teaspoon ground coriander

1 teaspoon ground fennel seeds

1 teaspoon ground caraway seeds

2 cloves

10 baby Lebanese (short) cucumbers, halved lengthways

salt and freshly ground black pepper

maple dressing

80 ml (2½ fl oz/⅓ cup) maple syrup

100 ml (3½ fl oz) extra-virgin olive oil

juice of 1 lemon

1 teaspoon ground cumin

enough for 6–8

For the pickled cucumbers, bring the vinegar and sugar to the boil in a saucepan, then simmer, stirring, until the sugar is dissolved. Pour the liquid into a large bowl and set aside to cool. When it has cooled, add the remaining ingredients, toss, season, cover and refrigerate.

Cook the quinoa in boiling, salted water until tender, about 10–15 minutes. Drain and set aside. Put the black rice in a large saucepan with 700 ml (24 fl oz) of water and bring to the boil over high heat. Add a pinch of salt – this will keep the husk of the grain firm – then reduce the heat to low and simmer until tender and all of the liquid has been absorbed into the rice, about 20–30 minutes. Remove from heat, add a splash of oil, stir and set aside to cool.

For the maple dressing, combine the maple syrup, oil, lemon juice and cumin in a large bowl.

Trim the tops off the baby carrots. Wash the tops and set aside to drain. Halve some of the carrots lengthways and quarter the rest. Gently toss the carrots in the bowl with the maple dressing, season and set aside.

Heat a chargrill pan over a medium–hot heat, brush with a little of the remaining oil, then grill the zucchini slices until nicely striped on both sides, season and set aside.

Place the rice and quinoa side by side in a large serving dish and top with the chargrilled zucchini, green beans, carrots and a drizzle of the maple dressing. Add the pickled cucumbers and splash a little of the pickled dressing on top and scatter with the carrot tops.

—

I've never been one to have a menu plan of what I'm going to cook, even when I owned a cafe it was always this way – spontaneous and fun with a touch of *manicomio* (madness).

vanna's angel voices cake

icing (confectioners') sugar, for dusting

custard

1 litre (34 fl oz/4 cups) full-cream (whole) milk

4 egg yolks

80 g (2¾ oz/⅓ cup) caster sugar

50 g (1¾ oz) cornflour (cornstarch)

rind of 1 lemon, cut into strips

pastry

125 g (4½ oz) unsalted butter, softened

150 g (5½ oz/⅔ cup) caster sugar

3 eggs

1 teaspoon natural vanilla extract

grated zest of 1 lemon

400 g (14 oz/2⅔ cups) plain (all-purpose) flour, plus extra for dusting

2 teaspoons baking powder

enough for 8

To make the custard, warm the milk in a saucepan over a low heat almost to boiling point, then set aside. Whisk the egg yolks, caster sugar and cornflour together briskly in a large bowl until well combined – the texture should be like smooth ricotta. Gradually pour the milk through a fine-mesh sieve into the egg mixture, whisking constantly. Wipe out the saucepan and pour the mixture back into it. Add the lemon rind and warm over a low heat, stirring intermittently with a balloon whisk, until it thickens, about 20 minutes. Scrape down the side of the pan as you go. Pour through the clean fine-mesh sieve into a bowl and set aside.

To make the pastry, beat the butter and sugar in the bowl of an electric mixer until pale. Add the eggs one at a time, beating after each addition until well incorporated. Add the vanilla and lemon zest and mix well. Sift the flour and baking powder together three times, then gradually fold them into the butter and sugar mixture. Divide the pastry (it's quite soft) into two rounds and cover them with cling wrap and refrigerate for 30 minutes.

Preheat the oven to 180°C (360°F). Before you grease the tin, trace its outline onto two sheets of baking paper, cut out the circles and set aside. Grease a 24 cm (9½ in) round non-stick springform tin with butter and line the base with baking paper.

Place one of the baking paper circles onto your bench and dust it with flour. Place one of the pastry rounds on top and dust it with flour. Place the other sheet of baking paper on top. Roll the pastry out between the two sheets until it reaches the size of the circle. Remove the top sheet, dust the pastry with a little more flour, then roll the pastry onto your rolling pin. Carefully unroll the pastry into the base of the prepared tin. Repeat with other pastry round to make a second pastry layer and set aside.

Pour the custard over the pastry base in the tin and carefully unroll the second pastry layer on top. Bake for 35–40 minutes, or until golden on top.

Allow the cake to cool completely in the tin before removing the springform side. Vanna's gorgeous cake doesn't need anything except for a light dusting of icing sugar.

This cake will keep for up to 2 days stored in an airtight container in the refrigerator.

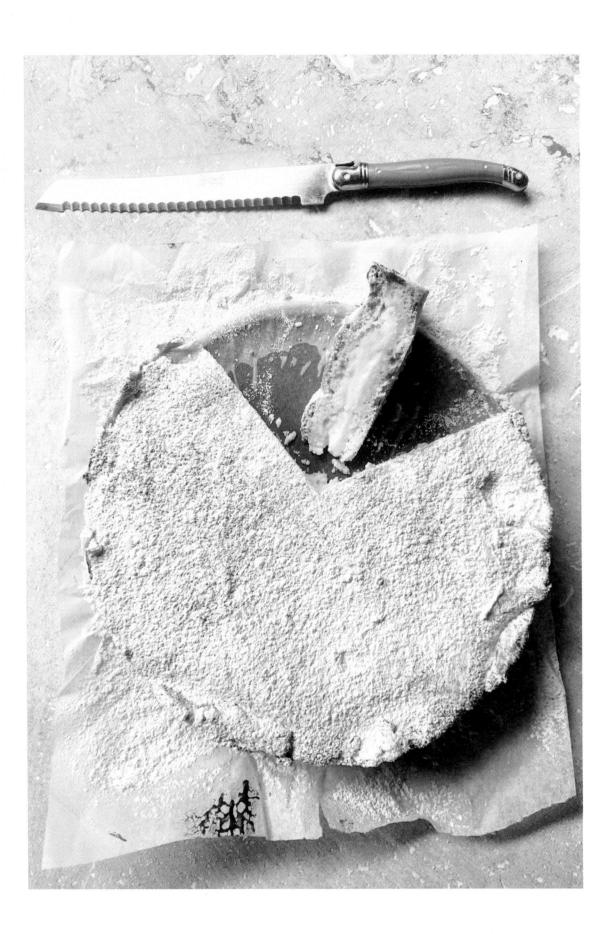

anzac cookies

300 g (10½ oz/2 cups) plain (all-purpose) flour

135 g (5 oz/1½ cups) desiccated (shredded) coconut

200 g (7 oz/2 cups) rolled (porridge) oats

80 g (2¾ oz/½ cup) sesame seeds

2 teaspoons ground ginger

95 g (3¼ oz/½ cup) soft brown sugar

95 g (3¼ oz/½ cup) dark muscovado sugar

250 g (9 oz) salted butter, chopped

2 tablespoons date syrup

½ teaspoon bicarbonate of soda (baking soda)

80 ml (2½ fl oz/⅓ cup) boiling water

makes 20

Preheat the oven to 170°C (340°F). Line a baking tray with baking paper.

Put the flour, coconut, oats, sesame seeds, ginger and both sugars in a large bowl and mix with your hands to combine.

Heat the butter and date syrup in a small saucepan over a low heat until melted and stir to combine. Put the bicarbonate of soda in a small bowl, add the boiling water and mix well. Add this to the melted butter mixture in the pan, it will fizz up a little, then pour it over the dry ingredients and stir to combine well.

Roll the mixture into balls about the size of an egg, then place them on the prepared baking tray. Use the palm of your hand to gently press down on the cookies to flatten them.

Bake the cookies for 15–20 minutes, or until golden. Allow them to cool on the tray for about 5 minutes before transferring to a wire rack to cool completely. I like a crisp Anzac, but if you prefer a chewy Anzac do not flatten them as much and cook for 12–15 minutes.

—

Diego, my father, and his younger brother Franco were too young to join the Italian army during the Second World War. Dad's older brothers Marco, Vincenzo and Michelle all fought in the war. The oldest of the brothers, Giuliano, was born in America in 1914, not long after Nonno and Nonna got married. A decade after the First World War, my grandparents returned to Sicily. At age fourteen, Giuliano returned to New York to start his life there and later joined the US army during the Second World War. After the war Nonno was anxious to leave Sicily and return to New York where Giuliano was living, but America didn't want them. Instead, my Sicilian family became among the first of two million immigrants from more than thirty European countries to arrive in Australia post–Second World War. One of my earliest memories is of my American Uncle Giuliano visiting us in the 1950s. Decades later when I visited him in Los Angelos, over a breakfast of fresh figs, prunes and toast with soft-boiled eggs, he expressed through tears his sadness at not being successful in sponsoring his family to move to the United States after the war.

citrus orchard cake with drunk dates

50 g (1¾ oz) pitted dates, diced

125 ml (4 fl oz/½ cup) dry marsala

250 ml (8½ fl oz/1 cup) grape seed oil

3 eggs

pinch of salt

grated zest of 1 lemon, 1 lime and 1 orange

125 g (4½ oz/½ cup) smooth ricotta

460 g (1 lb/2 cups) caster sugar

450 g (1 lb/3 cups) self-raising flour, sifted

2 mm (¹⁄₁₆ in) silver cachous, to decorate

citrus glaze

100 g (3½ oz/¾ cup) icing (confectioners') sugar

2 teaspoons each of lemon, lime and orange juice

enough for 6–8

Preheat the oven to 180°C (360°F). Grease a 24 cm (9½ in) angel cake tin with butter and line the centre tube with baking paper. Soak the dates in the marsala for 30 minutes.

Combine the oil, date mixture, eggs, salt, zests, ricotta and caster sugar in a large bowl and stir to mix well. Add the flour and stir to combine. Pour into the prepared tin and bake for 45–50 minutes, or until it tests done with a skewer. Remove from the oven and leave to cool in the tin completely. Once cool, gently turn the cake out onto a wire rack.

Meanwhile, to make the citrus glaze, combine the icing sugar and juices in a bowl. Whisk to a smooth, pourable glaze.

Transfer the cake to a serving plate, drizzle with citrus glaze and sprinkle on some cachous.

The cake will keep for up to 3–4 days stored in an airtight container in the refrigerator (bring to room temperature before serving).

—

I love everything about this cake and hope to continue to bake it for as long as I can. Sometimes I substitute the dates for dried apricots. In the autumn, when my local greengrocer has fresh dates available I use them to take this beautiful cake to another level. The same goes with fresh apricots.

sfinci

200 g (7 oz) new potatoes, peeled and
   cut into chunks

450 (1 lb/3 cups) self-raising flour, sifted

1 teaspoon baking powder

450 g (1 lb/2 cups) white (granulated) sugar

pinch of salt

2 litres (68 fl oz/8 cups) sunflower oil, for frying

makes about 40

Bring the potatoes to the boil with 1 litre (34 fl oz/4 cups) of water in a large saucepan, then reduce the heat to low and gently cook until soft, about 25 minutes. Let the potatoes cool a little in the water before blending with a hand-held blender to remove any lumps. Use a fork to stir in the flour, baking powder, 2 teaspoons of the sugar and the salt until just combined, then finish blending the mixture with the hand-held blender until it becomes thick. If you think your batter is too thick, add a little water. Let the batter rest for at least 1 hour.

I always use a wok to fry the *sfinci* – finding it to be the best when frying in batches – but if you don't have a wok, a medium pot of 17 cm (6¾ in) diameter will work. The oil should be almost 6 cm (2½ in) deep. Heat the oil to 180°C (360°F); any hotter and the *sfinci* will brown too quickly and be soggy in the middle. If you don't have a thermometer, test the heat by dropping a small amount of batter into the oil – if it sizzles, it's ready.

While you're waiting for the oil to heat up, line a large plate with paper towel and place it next to the stove. Fill a bowl with the remaining sugar and set aside.

Take a spoonful of *sfinci* batter and gently drop it into the oil. You can fry 8–10 at a time depending on the size of the wok or pot. When they turn golden underneath gently turn them over (I use two spoons for this). When the *sfinci* are golden brown all over, remove them with a slotted spoon and place them on the paper towel. Let them cool a little before rolling them in the sugar.

Once all the *sfinci* have been sugar-coated, place them on a serving dish and serve immediately.

———

There are so many grey areas between art, design and cooking. For me, the three collide in equal measure, providing the sanctuary I need to understand my various moods; to morph from one to the other. This fluid exchange began at Cumbrae Farm, where all my memories are awash with light. To leave the highway now and drive under the overhanging branches of McKirdys Road is like entering a Rick Amor painting – it seems real and yet it is more like a dream.

The footprint of the McKirdy's house demolition was left in the ground. The foundation of the hallway and four square rooms on either side became the borders of the new garden. The fragmented concrete back verandah became the link between the old and new. All the exterior and interior walls and the ceiling of our house were assembled entirely of recycled tongue-in-groove timber cladding. It created a patchwork of dark-stained timber, edged with peeling paint in various tints of greys and islands of red, matching the flamboyance of its post-war Sicilian migrants.

The new kitchen breathed life into what was essentially a house built of dust-encrusted wood and rusted corrugated iron with two disembodied front and back doors. You entered a large open-plan room centred with a dark wooden extension table with chunky cabriole legs. It was covered in baroque cloths, laden with a child's collection of coloured pencils and smelled of lead shavings, crayons and artworks that might one day arouse Florentine friends. The conversations, whispers, gestures, dreams, language and the endurance of this particular group of Sicilians, appeared all around this table.

Everyone lifting shared plates of *sfincione, pasta al forno*, locally caught squid, charred vegetables, meats and stuffed pork-skin ragu, cannoli and, of course, Bialetti-made cafeteria espresso.

The cypress's branches hung over the front entrance to the McKirdy's house, attracting a diversity of inhabitants surfing its limbs and meddling in the community of insects, finches and a melange of colourful birds of bright, red-carpet glitz and silk dupioni green. Sometimes the memories of childhood play tricks. Nevertheless, those early years shape us into who we are and the life we chose to live. I vividly remember the lilting hum and ever-present backdrop of daily worship to the Madonna del Giubino, the patron saint of Calatafimi. The prevailing mood in the house was interwoven with religious imagery of holy cards and the chant-chiming of words of death, adoration, forgiveness, love.

To the left of the enamelled Kooka was the open-mouthed fireplace, with portraits of Jesus, Mary, rosary beads, candles and little vases of flowers perched atop its mantelpiece.

Birthday and christening cakes were – and are still – bold and beautiful: whimsical towers of Italian torta with various pastel-coloured custards and sunshine, pale yellow frosting framed with a jubilant skirt of toasted bronze flaky almonds. We tuck in like Greek and Roman invaders riding elephants dressed in gold; feathers edged with silver baubles; cerulean leather saddles and tall, gilded umbrellas with shiny brush fringe trims in beige with deep red velvet and forest green tassels.

little ricotta cakes

375 g (13 oz) smooth ricotta

150 g (5½ oz/⅔ cup) caster sugar

4 eggs, separated

pinch of salt

½ teaspoon vanilla bean paste or
natural vanilla extract

grated zest and juice of 1 lemon

250 g (9 oz/2½ cups) almond flour

icing (confectioners') sugar, for dusting

makes 18 little cakes

Preheat the oven to 180°C (360°F). Use cupcake liners to line an 18-hole non-stick muffin tin to make 18 mini cakes (or you can use a 12-hole mini muffin tin and just bake the mixture in two batches to make eighteen cakes).

Combine the ricotta, caster sugar, egg yolks, salt, vanilla, lemon zest and juice in the bowl of an electric mixer and whisk on high speed until smooth. Reduce the speed to medium and gradually add the flour, a heaped spoonful at a time, whisking until smooth and scraping down the side of the bowl as you go.

In a different bowl, whisk the egg whites until they form soft peaks. Gently fold a third of the egg whites into the ricotta and almond batter. Add the remaining egg whites and fold until it is combined. Spoon the batter into the prepared muffin tin/s.

Bake for 20–25 minutes, or until golden brown on top. Let the cakes cool for 30 minutes, then remove them from the tin and cool for another 15 minutes. Dust with icing sugar to serve.

These little cakes are best eaten straight away, but they will keep for up to 3 days stored in an airtight container in the refrigerator.

———

I find it easier to take the cake out of the moulds if they're in paper cases. Just grip the baking paper at the top and they come out all in one go.

A young boy dreams of voyages by the great Spanish explorers sailing under grand amphitheatres of ribbed vaulted ceilings, which are imposing and awe-inspiring. They float above choir stalls of a stained-glass patchwork sky to the soundtrack of Handel's violins, exquisite colours of light showering over a Cumbrae night.

baci biscotti

180 g (6½ oz/2 cups) flaked almonds

200 g (7 oz/¾ cup) caster sugar

½ teaspoon ground cinnamon

¼ teaspoon freshly grated nutmeg

grated zest of 1 orange

3 egg whites, lightly whisked to combine

1 teaspoon natural pistachio extract

1 teaspoon natural almond extract

120 g (4½ oz/1 cup) pistachios, toasted

120 g (4½ oz/1 cup) walnuts, toasted

120 g (4½ oz/1 cup) hazelnuts, toasted

3 tablespoons sunflower kernels

3 tablespoons pepitas (pumpkin seeds)

200 g (7 oz/1 cup) dried apricots, chopped

ganache

200 g (7 oz) dark (70% cocoa) chocolate, chopped

200 ml (7 fl oz/¾ cup) thick cream (double/heavy)

1 tablespoon maple syrup

makes 24

To make the ganache, put the chocolate into a large heatproof bowl and set aside. Heat the cream in a small saucepan over a low heat until it comes to simmering point, then pour it over the chocolate. Do not stir. Cover with a tight fitting lid or cling wrap for 10 minutes, then stir well. Add the maple syrup and stir again. Strain the ganache into another bowl and allow it to cool overnight.

Preheat the oven to 180°C (360°F) and line a baking tray with baking paper.

Put the flaked almonds in a bowl and set aside. Put the sugar, cinnamon, nutmeg, orange zest, egg whites, pistachio and almond extracts in a large bowl and stir to combine.

Combine the remaining ingredients in a food processor and pulse until you have a course texture. Add the nut mixture to the bowl with the egg white mixture and stir to combine well.

Roll a tablespoon of biscotti mixture into a walnut-sized ball, then roll it in the flaked almonds. Push your thumb halfway into the centre of the ball to make a deep hole. Repeat until all the mixture is used.

Bake the biscotti on the baking tray for around 15 minutes, or until light golden. Leave to cool on the tray. Once cool, spoon a little ganache into the centre of each biscotti. As an alternative, fill with a little dollop of apricot jam.

These biscotti will keep for up to a week stored in an airtight container.

The painting of Isola Bella opposite was the only picture hanging in our house besides prints of Mary, Jesus and the Apostles. It was taken to the cafe and now hangs in my studio. For me, the framed Doors album evokes the power of the gilt-framed *Last Supper* floating next to Isola Bella at Cumbrae. Isola Bella, a small island near Taormina, was the property of Lady Florence Trevelyan and her husband Salvatore Cacciola, a local doctor and mayor of Taormina. After her death, Isola Bella remained in private ownership until 1990. It is maintained and protected as a natural reserve by the World Wide Fund for Nature and the Sicilian Regional Government.

After many years of working in graphics and cooking, I am still flabbergasted at the sensation, excitement, relief and the emotional affect it has on me. The luxuriating blackness of clouds of squid ink to colour and flavour spaghetti; the dark-night pigment always touches my heart, reminding me of Sunday *pranzo* at Cumbrae Farm with its still-life scenes of tantalising shades of affection. It is served with recollections over many years, above a myriad of light and whispers, there is the sense of being complete while losing control.

Last night I dreamt of my boyhood, Cumbrae Farm, beautiful people with beautiful problems, climbing bridges under Western Port Bay, sea monsters, sitting on rainbows under late-afternoon storms. Horned leopards stood at the entrance to a long gallery with phosphorescent marine-green walls. A crowded universe of racing impalas trying to get away from their phones and computers. Sicilian dialects of all kinds joined a bunch of arty types pursuing eloquent, expressive adventures, saying words like *agghiu*, *cori*, *famigghia*, *guardari* and *zuccaru*.

I make no apology for the memories I hold of my childhood between the ages of seven and fourteen. It was another time, another place that is so vivid in my mind still. How fortunate I was to have been surrounded by so much love and so much cooking. Ageing is just a word; I still feel that same sense of wonder and curiosity. As I get older there is still so much to explore. Isola Bella and Segesta are like porcelain memories for me now, tender and fragile, leaping out every now and then from behind closed doors to remind this old man of the gift and battles of youth.

index

grazie

Grazie to Roxy Ryan, for taking the little black briefcase tied with a red ribbon and having the conviction to open it. Simon Davis, for seeing me as I am and gently pushing forward and for believing like me that more is more. Your determined eye and enthusiasm turned the original concept into a jewel box. Jasmin Chua, who kept the experience alive and kept everything on course with patience and encouragement. Martine Lleonart, for the delicate treatment to words and character. Celia Mance, for translating my Quark files into the modern world of InDesign without loss of translation from the original. Lisa Bayley, who introduced me to the history of the McKirdy family at Cumbrae. Thank you all for your hard work.

Thank you to my parents Diego and Pina and my Nonno Gaetano and Nonna Giuseppa (Giovanna), who from a young age saw a passion in me for art, a love of food and cooking and for putting up with a grumpy little boy at Cumbrae, and introducing me to all things Sicilian. I am filled with gratitude for all the love you gave. I wish you were still here.

My siblings, Frank, Josie and Rosa in providing my memory with light when it became foggy. I am grateful to my cousins Vittoria, Josie, Vanna and Zia Franca, whose knowledge of our home cooking provided me with essential insight into the whole Sicilianish thing.

Cafe life was in my blood like holy water. I was blessed with the most dear staff who inspired me at every moment. While I was missing in action for many days during the making of *Pranzo*, this extraordinary group of talented women and men kept the pots simmering, the coffee machine pumping, the customers happy and tolerated my absences and constant 'book talk'. I am endlessly grateful and enamoured of you. I'm listing you all in alphabetical order like the last 'Super contributions summary' sent to me by my amazing bookkeeper Christie Gunn: Raechel Adams, Amanda Brandon, Benjamin Canavan, So Yun Chong, Susan Dixon, Melanie Elston (also known as Melanie Russo), Ethan Naylor, Holly-Mae Seager, Jemima Stocker, Joe Stocker, Ruby Stocker, Angus James Taylor, Sade-Simona Tobich, Giuseppe (Joe) Trinchi, Kristopher Wheatley. Thank you so much to all our loyal customers who became part of the fabric and daily conversation; if you're reading this, you know who you are. I am incredibly fortunate to have 'crossed the road' to get to know you all.

To my talented, fun and special family: Danielle, Donna, Pam, Chris, Paul, Jess and my gorgeous grandbabies Raphael, Theodore, Otto and Leni. Your enthusiasm, patience and love of food and cooking helped keep this book alive. Danielle, your knowledge of the book business and guidance through the making of *Pranzo* balanced the flavours beautifully.

And lastly … Johanne (also known as Jojo). It was you who really started this. Marriage to you is like a serene act in the steps of a tango. The pleasure of feeling blood pouring through our veins, a shortness of breath, an arm around the waist, a hand on the shoulder. I am indebted to you for so much. Thank you for waiting to eat while I take the photo, and for putting up with the chaos and mess. And for enduring a grumpy old man.

In 1888 Alexander and Emily McKirdy took possession of crown land portion 58 in Tyabb, located on the land of the traditional owners, the Bunurong people, on the edge of Bagge Harbour, Western Port Bay. Alexander emigrated from Scotland in 1856 and married Emily Norket in 1859 at Beechworth, Victoria. They had ten children and had relocated from Castlemaine to Tyabb to be near Emily's sister Jane, who was living in Somerville. The farm was named 'Cumbrae' after the Scottish island where Alexander was born in 1824. Emily was born in Horsham, Sussex, England in 1837. They planted apple, pear and stone fruit orchards, had a drove of sheep, goats, Jersey dairy cattle, pigs, chooks and ducks.

—

In 1959 Diego and Pina Mirabella took possession of Cumbrae Farm. Diego emigrated from Sicily in 1949, Pina followed in 1951. They planted potatoes, pumpkin (winter squash), tomatoes and broccoli beside new orchards of apple, pear and stone fruit, a drove of sheep, goats, Jersey dairy cattle, pigs, chooks and ducks with the odd geese or two.

About the author

Guy Mirabella is one of Australia's most celebrated book designers, renowned for his iconic cookbooks of the 1990s by culinary luminaries such as Stephanie Alexander, Christine Manfield and Charmaine Solomon. In 2002, he opened the beloved Shop Ate Cafe & Store in Mount Eliza on the Mornington Peninsula, where he nurtured a vibrant community hub for two decades before selling the business in December 2022. Guy's Sicilian heritage profoundly influences his cooking, with recipes that celebrate the robust, seasonal flavours of his upbringing on a small peninsula farm, where his parents settled after leaving postwar Europe.

Published in 2025 by Hardie Grant Books, an imprint of Hardie Grant Publishing

Hardie Grant Books (Melbourne)
Wurundjeri Country
Building 1, 658 Church Street
Richmond, Victoria 3121

Hardie Grant North America
2912 Telegraph Ave
Berkeley, California 94705

hardiegrant.com/books

Hardie Grant acknowledges the Traditional Owners of the Country on which we work, the Wurundjeri People of the Kulin Nation and the Gadigal People of the Eora Nation, and recognises their continuing connection to the land, waters and culture. We pay our respects to their Elders past and present.

 A catalogue record for this book is available from the National Library of Australia

Pranzo: Sicilian(ish) Recipes & Stories
ISBN 978 1 76145 090 7
ISBN 978 1 76145 091 4 (ebook)

10 9 8 7 6 5 4 3 2 1

Designer, Photographer and Stylist: Guy Mirabella

Publisher: Simon Davis
Head of Editorial: Jasmin Chua
Editor: Martine Lleonart
Creative Director: Kristin Thomas
Typesetter: Celia Mance
Head of Production: Todd Rechner
Production Controller: Jessica Harvie

Colour reproduction by Splitting Image Colour Studio
Printed in China by Leo Paper Products LTD.